Preparing to Meet Jesus

Preparing
to Meet Jesus

A 21-Day Challenge
to Move from Salvation
to Transformation

Anne Graham Lotz
and
Rachel-Ruth Lotz Wright

Published in the United States by Multnomah, an imprint of Random House, a division of Penguin Random House LLC.

MULTNOMAH is a registered trademark and the M colophon is a trademark of Penguin Random House LLC.

Published in association with the literary agency of Alive Literary Agency, 5001 Centennial Blvd., No. 50742, Colorado Springs, CO 80908, www.aliveliterary.com.

Library of Congress Cataloging-in-Publication Data
Names: Lotz, Anne Graham, author. | Wright, Rachel-Ruth Lotz, author.
Title: Preparing to meet Jesus: a 21-day challenge to move from salvation to transformation / Anne Graham Lotz and Rachel-Ruth Lotz Wright.
Description: First edition. | Colorado Springs, Colorado: Multnomah, [2023] | Includes bibliographical references.
Identifiers: LCCN 2022055935 | ISBN 9780525651956 (hardcover; acid-free paper) | ISBN 9780525652281 (ebook)
Subjects: LCSH: Spiritual life—Christianity—Meditations.
Classification: LCC BV4501.3 .L675 2023 |
DDC 242—dc23/eng/20230217
LC record available at https://lccn.loc.gov/2022055935

Printed in Canada on acid-free paper

waterbrookmultnomah.com

4 6 8 9 7 5 3

Book design by Susan Turner

Most Multnomah books are available at special quantity discounts for bulk purchase for premiums, fundraising, and corporate and educational needs by organizations, churches, and businesses. Special books or book excerpts also can be created to fit specific needs. For details, contact specialmarketscms@penguinrandomhouse.com.

Dedicated
to
Jesus Followers

Hallelujah!
For our Lord God Almighty reigns.
Let us rejoice and be glad
and give him glory!
For the wedding of the Lamb has come,
and his bride has made herself ready.

Revelation 19:6–7

CONTENTS

Contents

Preparing to Meet Jesus

INTRODUCTION

The One the Father Seeks

JESUS IS COMING! ALL INDICATORS POINT TO THE FACT that His return is imminent. While expectancy among people of faith worldwide is at a fever pitch, I wonder if you and I are actually prepared for that world-changing, history-altering, heart-stopping moment in time?

Again and again, the Bible tells us that Jesus will come suddenly . . . quickly . . . like a thief in the night . . . and that His followers need to be prepared to meet Him at any moment.

I became a follower of Jesus when I was a young girl. In response to a movie depicting His life, I knelt by my bed in prayer. I knew with deep conviction that the horror of the Cross I had just watched portrayed on television was my fault. Jesus had died in order to take away my sin and forgive me for all the wrong things I had done. I was acutely aware that if I had been the only sinner in need of saving, He would still have died just for me. So in fear and trembling, I told Him I was sorry for my sin, asked for His forgiveness, and invited Him to come into my heart.

While I was too young to understand the full ramifications of that decision, I had an immediate sense of relief, peace, and joy, as though a burden had been lifted, one I hadn't realized I was carrying. With a heart full of love and gratitude for the One who died for me, I began a lifelong journey to know Him, to serve Him, to obey Him, to please Him, to follow Him, to glorify Him more fully every day.

Now, not only because of my age but also as world events line up with the signs Jesus gave us to indicate we are living at the end of human history, I know with certainty that I will soon meet Him face-to-face. I live on the tiptoe of expectancy that at any moment I might see the One "who loved me and gave himself for me."[1] And I believe that He, too, is filled with eager anticipation as He looks forward to meeting the bride His Father has sought for Him.

The Subject of the Search

What comes to mind as you consider your relationship with Jesus? Did you know that He's not looking to see how well you follow a list of dos and don'ts? Did you know that a genuine connection with Him transcends denominations and organizations and traditions and rituals? Did you know that it's about an intimate love relationship, like the one between a bridegroom and his bride? In fact, the Bible refers to followers of Jesus as His bride.

Like any bride, I'm a little nervous about meeting the Bridegroom.

I remember the day I married Danny Lotz. My father, who never came upstairs to my bedroom, suddenly appeared in the doorway. He sat on the bed beside me as I told him how nervous and fearful I was. Would Danny find me pleasing? He was almost twelve years older than I was. He had waited a long time to get married. Would I be all he had been longing for in a bride? My father assured me that I would; then he put his arms around me and prayed for me. God answered that prayer. When we met later that evening at the altar, the smile on Danny's face stretched almost from ear to ear!

While I'm eager to see Jesus in person, once again I find myself a little nervous. He has waited a very long time for the wedding. What will that first face-to-face moment be like? Will I be all that He has been looking for . . . longing for . . . in a bride? Will I be pleasing to Him?

That question is of such critical significance that I don't want to leave anything to chance. I want to be ready. I want to prepare now to meet Jesus.

What about you? As you consider meeting Him, what hopes and fears surface from the recesses of your heart? Do you wonder whether He'll be pleased or disappointed as His eyes fall on you? What will be the expression on His face when He sees you? Do you even know what He is looking for in a bride?

If you are a male reader, while you recognize Jesus as your Savior, your dearest Friend, your divine Companion, and your Lord and Master, it may seem a little off-putting to think of Him as your Bridegroom. Let me put you at ease. This is the way He described Himself.[2] Jesus used this term to underscore the fact that our relationship with Him is a love relationship, and the Bible uses the analogy of marriage to describe our relationship with Jesus. Following a well-known passage about marriage, Ephesians 5:32 reveals, "This is a profound mystery—but I am talking about Christ and the church." The church—not the organized church that assembles in buildings, but the collective followers of Jesus—is His bride.

Each of us enters into this relationship when we put our trust in Jesus at the "marriage altar" of the Cross. So whether male or female, Jew or Gentile, rich or poor, weak or strong, young or old, we are each invited to come to the altar, say yes to Jesus, make our vow of commitment to honor, obey, and love Him as long as we live, then enjoy life as the bride of the Son of God, looking forward with eager expectancy to the wedding supper of the Lamb.[3]

THE INITIATIVE

To be clear, God the Father will not settle for just any bride for His Son. He's looking for one that is holy, cleansed of sin, and at peace with Him.[4] This search for the bride of His choice is illustrated by a beautiful story recorded in Genesis 24 that describes the effort one father made to find the perfect bride for his beloved son. And although the story is a true one, it is also an incredible analogy of our heavenly Father, who has made the supreme effort to find the perfect bride for His Son.

The Genesis account tells of Abraham, whose son Isaac would one day inherit the unique promises, blessings, and covenant relationship with God that had been given to Abraham. As a godly father, Abraham knew it was of preeminent importance that his son have a godly wife. So he took the initiative to search for one.

I have to smile as I remember the initiative my own father took to find a godly husband for me. The first week of the summer following my graduation from high school, I was free to go out, which I did. Every night. With the same guy. Daddy, who happened to be home at the time rather than traveling as he often did, became alarmed. He knew that the Fellowship of Christian Athletes was having its annual conference across the valley from our home, so he placed a call to the national director and asked if there was a Christian athlete who would take me to one of their meetings. The result? On the last night of the conference, I went to the closing meeting with Danny Lotz. He was the son of a New York City preacher, had won the NCAA basketball championship on an undefeated team at the University of North Carolina, had finished dental school, and was a captain in the air force whose commander allowed him to volunteer for all the FCA summer conferences.

Because my father had arranged for this date, I didn't take it seriously, which meant I was very relaxed. I didn't try to impress Danny in the least. What I found interesting was that we were very comfortable with each other. As we talked, we discovered that we enjoyed the same type of music and the same kinds of foods. But most important, we shared the same faith, which became very apparent at the FCA event. We were led in lively worship, and I was thrilled by the sound of about eight hundred male athletes all singing at the top of their lungs, accentuating their music by stomping their feet and clapping their hands. Then we listened to testimonies given by well-known professional and college athletes. All in all, it was a thoroughly enjoyable evening. Since Danny returned the next morning to Holloman Air Force Base in New Mexico, I thought that was that.

About one month after our initial date, Danny came to visit on leave. Once again, my father was home, and he and Danny seemed to really hit it off. By contrast, I was still somewhat uninterested, primarily because of Danny's age and the fact I was headed to college that fall.

My third meeting with Danny was in Denver, Colorado. I had been at a leadership training institute in California and stopped in Denver to see Daddy and attend the crusade he was holding there. Danny, who had just completed his military commitment and been discharged from the air force, drove up from New Mexico to meet me.

We spent the day together touring the spectacular Rockies nearby; then Danny drove me back to my hotel. As we enjoyed an ice cream soda in the hotel coffee shop, I was taken aback when Danny told me he was in love with me and wanted to marry me. This was our third date! I told him I couldn't care less. He asked if he could pursue the relationship, and I told him it was a free country so he could do what he wanted, but I wasn't going to encourage him.

Afterward I went straight to my father's room and told him what Danny had said. I thought for sure he would pick up the phone and tell Danny it was time for him to leave. Instead, Daddy looked at me and said, "Anne, I think Danny Lotz is the man you are going to marry." Talk about a shock! But deep down, while I can't explain why, I knew what Daddy said was right. A little more than a year later, Danny and I were married, entering into a relationship that lasted until his death forty-nine years later. I will always be grateful that Daddy took the initiative to find a godly man for me.

While I don't necessarily recommend fathers doing what mine did, I can appreciate why Abraham took the initiative to find a godly wife for his son Isaac. Single-ness wasn't an option for Isaac, since God had prom-ised Abraham a multitude of descendants through Isaac, who was uniquely the son of promise. This im-plied that Isaac would have children and therefore would need a wife. But Abraham and Isaac lived in the land of the Canaanites, wicked people given over to obscene, pornographic behavior. Where could a godly woman be found for Isaac to marry? The people who came to Abraham's mind were his own extended fam-ily, who lived in Haran, more than 450 miles away.[5]

Since Abraham was too old for such a long journey, he made a bold decision and called for "the chief ser-vant in his household, the one in charge of all that he had."[6] While we can't be certain, it seems likely that this is Eliezer, the servant who would have inherited Abraham's estate had there been no natural descendant.[7]

THE INSTRUCTIONS

When the servant answered Abraham's summons, he received not the customary gracious greeting but a very solemn charge: "I want you to swear by the LORD, the God of heaven and the God of earth, that you will not get a wife for my son from the daughters of the Canaanites, among whom I am living, but will go to my country and my own relatives and get a wife for my son Isaac."[8]

The servant responded by respectfully asking a logical question: "What if the woman is unwilling to come back with me to this land? Shall I then take your son back to the country you came from?"[9] It would seem highly improbable that a young woman suited to be Isaac's wife would accept a proposal presented by the servant of an unknown relative and forsake her friends, her father's house, her country, and all that was familiar, and travel hundreds of miles to marry someone she knew nothing about.

But Abraham didn't waver. He assured the servant that God would "send his angel before you so that you can get a wife for my son from there."[10] Abraham was completely confident that God would help the servant on this critical mission, because he was confident that God also wanted a godly wife for his son. As the heir to God's promises and God's covenant, Isaac needed a suitable helper in raising a godly son who would also inherit the covenant blessings. If the servant found the woman and for any reason she was unwilling to accept Abraham's offer of his son, then the servant was released from his obligation and his oath to bring her back.[11]

When Abraham had finished giving the instructions, his servant "took ten of his master's camels and left, taking with him all kinds of good things from his master"—gold, jewelry, linens, silks, spices, and other costly items.[12] Once the servant found the right person, he'd need to make the absent bridegroom attractive to her, so he planned to shower her with gifts to give her some idea of the greatness and wealth of the son and his father.

The Significance of the Search

After a long journey through desert wasteland, bandit territory, and rock-strewn wilderness, the servant finally arrived in the city of Nahor, a suburb of Haran. Fully committed to his task, the servant wasted no time. He went to the city well and had his camels kneel down.[13] He knew there was no better place to find the woman he was seeking than where women gathered each evening to draw water for their households.

THE PLACE

While the well was a literal, physical place to draw water, it also has symbolic significance. The Bible describes many divine meetings that took place at a well.[14] The Lord met Hagar at a well when she was running away from Abraham's wife, Sarah. There He established a personal relationship with her. Later, when Hagar was on the desert road after leaving Abraham's household with her son, Ishmael, the Lord provided water from a well and promised to bless her and her son.[15] Abraham's grandson Jacob met the love of his life, Rachel, at a well, where he promptly kissed her.[16] While fleeing from Pharaoh, Moses sat down at a well, where he met his future wife.[17] Beside a well, Gideon heard from God, who commanded him to reduce his army of thirty-two thousand men to three hundred before they were given victory over the invading enemy.[18]

But perhaps the most meaningful of these events took place at Jacob's well in Samaria. In the heat of the noonday sun, a travel-weary Jesus encountered a woman who had come to draw water. He asked her for a drink. In the resulting conversation, Jesus revealed that physical water doesn't satisfy the thirst of the heart and soul. He then clearly stated that anyone who drank the water He offered would never thirst again, because "the water I give him will become in him a spring of water welling up to eternal life."[19] Later, Scripture makes clear that the water He was referring to was the indwelling life of the Holy Spirit.[20] The woman was amazed! She ran to tell those who lived in her city that she had met the Messiah, and the entire population came out to the well to meet Him.[21]

Life-changing well encounters still occur today. The prophet Isaiah exclaimed, "With joy you will draw water from the wells of salvation."[22] When we place our faith in Jesus as Savior and Lord and receive Him into our hearts in the person of the Holy Spirit, we also are receiving through Him the well of living water Jesus described to the Samaritan woman. A spring wells up in us, bringing joy, peace, love, hope, and what I would describe as a vibrancy to life itself.

The well can also symbolize a place to meet with other followers of Jesus, where God does significant things in our lives. It's striking to me that my parents met each other at the "well" of a prayer meeting. My husband's parents met at the "well" of a church service. I met my husband at the "well" of a Fellowship of Christian Athletes meeting. My two daughters also each met their husbands at the "well" of FCA.

Just as Abraham's servant knew that the best way to find Isaac's bride was to be where the women gathered, if we want to experience life-giving relationships with those who will help us love Jesus more fully and trust Him more completely, we need to put ourselves, our children, and our grandchildren in a place where we can meet other followers of Jesus, such as at a Bible study, church, Christian youth group, or fellowship meetings. This is true not only in our quest for trustworthy, lifelong friends but also in the search for a godly spouse.

The Prayer

As he waited at the well after his long journey, the servant prayed with great humility and expectancy: "O Lord, God of my master Abraham, give me success today, and show kindness to my master Abraham. See, I am standing beside this spring, and the daughters of the townspeople are coming out to draw water. May it be that when I say to a girl, 'Please let down your jar that I may have a drink,' and she says, 'Drink, and I'll water your camels too'—let her be the one you have chosen for your servant Isaac. By this I will know that you have shown kindness to my master."[23]

The servant's request was somewhat unreasonable. Many young women who came to draw water would probably have given a drink to a hot, dusty, thirsty traveler if he asked. But it would have been al-most beyond imagination for anyone to offer to water his camels also, unless God intervened and moved her heart to do so.

The spring of water on the outskirts of Nahor most likely was located within a well that was accessed by a circular stairway. Whoever watered the camels would have to walk down the steps, fill the bucket with water, walk back up the steps, pour it into the watering trough, turn around, go back down the steps, fill the bucket, go back up the steps, pour it out—again and again and again. Camels can drink up to thirty gallons of water each. The servant was praying for a girl who would be willing not only to get the water she needed for herself but also to spend at least an hour of hard work getting water for his ten camels!

Before the servant had even finished praying, God answered. A beautiful young woman caught his eye. He "hurried to meet her and said, 'Please give me a little water from your jar.'"[24] Then she offered, "I'll draw water for your camels too, until they have fin-ished drinking."[25] What an amazing response! Surely God Himself had moved her to make such an offer.

When finally the last camel had satisfied its thirst, the servant took out a gold ring and heavy gold bracelets to give the young woman in appreciation for what she had done. He knew the time had come to take the next step, so he inquired, "Whose daughter are you? Please tell me, is there room in your father's house for us to spend the night?"[26] He knew it wasn't enough to find a phenomenally beautiful, hardworking girl for Isaac. She also needed to be from a God-fearing family.

Rebekah's straightforward yet astounding response confirmed the answer to his prayer: "I am the daughter of Bethuel, the son that Milcah bore to Nahor."[27] Nahor was Abraham's brother! This girl who had offered him a drink, then watered all his camels, was from the very family to which his master Abraham had directed him! There was no doubt. This was the girl he had come to find.

THE PRAISE

The servant must have fallen to the ground in amazement and awe and unrestrained worship. "Praise be to the LORD, the God of my master Abraham," he declared, "who has not abandoned his kindness and faithfulness to my master. As for me, the LORD has led me on the journey to the house of my master's relatives."[28]

When the servant finished praising God and rose from the ground, he discovered that Rebekah had disappeared! But he didn't frantically search for her. He simply waited, knowing that if God had brought her to him once, God could bring her to him again. He didn't have to wait long.

Rebekah had run back home to tell her family about a remarkable man who had given her some spectacular and valuable jewelry. When her brother, Laban, saw the expensive gifts, his eyes must have lit up. As we know from later encounters, he was a conniving, shrewd man. He "hurried out to the man at the spring" and found the servant "standing by the camels near the spring," obviously waiting patiently for the next step in God's plan to unfold.[29]

As he greeted the servant, Laban gushed, "Come, you who are blessed by the LORD. . . . Why are you standing out here? I have prepared the house and a place for the camels."[30] Abraham's servant accepted the gracious offer of hospitality and followed Laban to the house. The camels were unloaded and fed, a bath was prepared for the servant and for the men who had traveled with him, and refreshments were presented. Through it all, the servant patiently waited to tell his story. But he didn't wait too long.

THE PRIORITY

When the food was set before him, he resisted: "I will not eat until I have told you what I have to say."[31] As he recounted his story, the servant didn't focus on himself. First he spoke of the greatness of Abraham, the father: "The LORD has blessed my master abundantly, and he has become wealthy. He has given him sheep

and cattle, silver and gold, menservants and maidser-
vants, and camels and donkeys."[32] Then he spoke of
Isaac as the only beloved son of the father, to whom
Abraham had promised everything he owned.[33] The
servant described Abraham and Isaac in such glowing
terms that although they weren't physically present,
those listening must have been irresistibly drawn to
them.

With Rebekah and her family hanging on every
word, the servant explained how Abraham had en-
trusted him with the task of finding a bride for Isaac,
declaring, "You must not get a wife for my son from the
daughters of the Canaanites . . . but go to my father's
family and to my own clan, and get a wife for my son."[34]
As the servant recalled Abraham's words, the tone of
his voice must have conveyed the seriousness with
which he had accepted the responsibility for this overwhelming task.

I wonder if his face broke into a warm smile at the
memory of Abraham's encouraging words of faith that
had given birth to genuine expectancy in his heart:
"The LORD, before whom I have walked, will send his
angel with you and make your journey a success."[35]
Rebekah's family must have noticed the sparkle of excitement in his eyes as he began to unfold for them his
side of the meeting at the well. He described how he
had come to the spring, how he had prayed specifically

for God to give him success by leading him to the bride for Isaac, how even before he had finished praying, he had looked up and seen Rebekah! His admiring gaze must have turned to her as he related their interaction and how she had become the dramatic answer to his prayer.

The Presentation

With bold assurance, the servant stated that he knew God had led him "on the right road to get the grand-daughter of my master's brother for his son."[36] Every-one who had gathered around to listen was convinced of the servant's certainty that Rebekah was God's choice of a bride for Isaac. The servant concluded by presenting the family with a choice: "If you will show kindness and faithfulness to my master, tell me; and if not, tell me, so I may know which way to turn."[37]

Laban, Rebekah's brother, and Bethuel, her father, spoke in total unity. "This is from the LORD," they said. "Here is Rebekah; take her and go, and let her become the wife of your master's son, as the LORD has di-rected."[38]

Overcome once again with gratitude to God, the servant immediately "bowed down to the ground be-fore the LORD."[39] His words had been received; his mission had been understood; the offer had been ac-cepted. He had no words to express how he felt, only the intensely meaningful and poignant gesture of humble worship.

The Success of the Search

The servant then stepped over to the big, heavy packs he had brought such a long way, opened them up, and distributed gifts of sparkling jewels and gleaming gold and silver necklaces, bracelets, and rings, along with shimmering silks, fine linen clothing, and other costly treasures for Rebekah and her family. So many extravagant gifts! And such a variety! The gifts indicated that Abraham was wealthier than their wildest dreams. Surely the abundance and the extravagance of these treasures confirmed the decision Laban and Bethuel had made for Rebekah to become Isaac's bride.

But the wise servant hadn't yet heard from Rebekah. She hadn't indicated her choice. I wonder if the display of gifts was partially his way of persuading her, without pressure. He was giving her just a glimpse of what would one day be hers if she chose to be Isaac's bride.

The Success Depends on Our Choice

The next morning Laban suggested the servant's return journey be delayed for ten days so that Rebekah could have more time at home. The wise servant insisted, "Do not detain me, now that the LORD has granted success to my journey. Send me on my way so I may go to my master."[40] He knew the decision needed to be made at that moment, then promptly acted on. Any postponement would only make room for indecision on Rebekah's part, as well as provide opportunity for her brother and father to reconsider their decision to let her go.

"They called Rebekah and asked her, 'Will you go with this man?'"[41] Rebekah had to choose for herself. In fact, it was the only way she could become Isaac's bride. The servant would never have accepted a forced arrangement. He wanted her to come with him and choose life with Isaac of her own free will.

Rebekah replied, "I will go."[42]

THE SUCCESS DEPENDS ON OUR COMMITMENT

Once Rebekah made the decision, her family blessed her. "Then Rebekah and her maids got ready and mounted their camels and went back with the man. So the servant took Rebekah and left."[43] The servant had to transport Rebekah back over the difficult and dangerous route to Canaan. It was his responsibility to protect her and guard her and keep her and deliver her safely to Isaac. It was Rebekah's responsibility to live out her commitment to be Isaac's bride as she allowed the servant to lead her step by step. Mile by mile. Day after day. Week after week.

As monotonous as the desert view likely was, the mounting anticipation must have been almost palpable. Without a doubt, Rebekah was consumed with thoughts of Isaac.

The servant must have thoroughly enjoyed talking to the beautiful young woman about the greatness of the father and the glory of the son. He must have told Rebekah about Isaac's miraculous conception and birth.[44] He may have told her about Ishmael's jealousy of Isaac, his voice dropping as he described the painful scene of Ishmael's removal from the home.[45] And did he tell her about Mount Moriah, where Isaac was spared death at the last moment because God had said he would provide a lamb to die on the altar in his place?[46]

As Rebekah learned more and more about Isaac, she must have fallen in love with him before she even saw him. She must have longed for him and begun to look for him, especially as she knew her journey was coming to an end and she was drawing near to the place where he was.

As I journey through life on my way to the Father's house, the Holy Spirit, who is the Holy Servant, is teaching me about the Father's Son.[47] He has told me . . .

  . . . about His miraculous conception and birth.[48]

  . . . about His life on earth.[49]

. . . about His sacrifice on the cross when the Father provided His own Son as the Lamb.[50]

. . . about His resurrection.[51]

. . . about His ascension into Heaven.[52]

I have learned that He is the Father's sole heir[53] and that, as His bride, I will share in His wealth and power and glory.[54] The Holy Spirit has shown me a vast variety of gifts from which He's carefully selected specific ones to give me in the name of the Son.[55] I have learned that the Son is seated at the Father's right hand, thinking of me and praying for me right now.[56] And I have been told that He is looking for me! That one day I will look up and see Him coming to receive me to Himself so that I can live with Him in His heavenly Home forever.[57] It's no wonder that even though I have yet to see Him visibly, I already love Him! I believe in Him. And I'm filled with inexpressible and glorious joy at the very thought of Him.[58]

As my journey draws to an end—whether because I'm growing older or because the time for His return is near—my expectation of seeing Jesus is intensifying. I long to see the expression on His face when He sees me . . . and my children and grandchildren. I long to hear the sound of His voice speaking my name. And I long to feel His touch. My anticipation of being physically in His presence is at times almost a tangible ache.

In a similar way, Rebekah's anticipation must have

reached a crescendo. After weeks of travel, on an evening that probably looked like many previous ones, her attention was caught by movement. Instinctively, she knew. It was Isaac. He was coming for her! This encounter was the climax of her entire journey. She hastily slipped off the camel; then just to make sure, she asked the servant, "Who is that man in the field coming to meet us?"[59] Her hope was confirmed when he answered, "He is my master."[60]

THE SUCCESS DEPENDS ON OUR CONSTANCY

I wonder if it suddenly occurred to Rebekah that while she had been learning all about Isaac, he knew nothing about her. I wonder if she was in love with him but feared he wouldn't love her. Would she be pleasing in his eyes? Would she be what he was looking for and longing for? Would she be all he expected her to be? She knew Isaac was the father's sole heir. As his bride, she would share in all that was his. She was walking toward one who would transform her life with vast wealth and power and position. But would their marriage be only an official arrangement? Or would their relationship be one of genuine love? She seemed overcome with shyness, so she took her veil and covered herself.[61]

Before long, Isaac's response would lay all Rebekah's fears to rest. He had gone out into the field to meditate, but I wonder if he had been watching for her too. After forty years of singleness, his mind must have been filled with thoughts of his bride, who she would be and what she would be like. As she drew near, he, too, must have felt his heart skip a beat! Since she was veiled, all he would have been able to see was a female form swathed in the fine linen clothing his father had provided for her. Would he be pleased? Or would he be disappointed?

There must have been introductions then, as Isaac and Rebekah gazed on each other for the first time and "the servant told Isaac all he had done."[62] How thrilled the servant must have been to present the bride to Abraham's son and explain all that God had orchestrated to make this moment possible. She was exactly the bride the father had sought for his son. But would she be what Isaac wanted? The Bible leaves no room for doubt: "Isaac brought her into the tent of his mother Sarah, and he married Rebekah. So she became his wife, and he loved her."[63]

The Bible doesn't tell us what Abraham thought about his new daughter-in-law. But I know. Without any doubt, he loved her because she loved his son.

If you ever wonder what the heavenly Father thinks about you, just remember this: Love His Son, and you can be absolutely reassured that the Father loves you.[64]

Not only is Abraham's parental leadership exemplary, but it also beautifully parallels the heavenly Father's desire to secure a bride for His Son. Just as Abraham sent his servant to look for a godly match, God the Father sends His Spirit into the world to find a fitting bride for His Son. But the choice of whether or not to "go with this man" is ours. Once we decide to be the one the Father seeks, we must follow through with a commitment that results not in a 450-mile trip but in a lifelong journey of faith. And every step of the way, the Father's Servant, the Holy Spirit, will guide, protect, instruct, and strengthen us until the glorious day when He presents us to the Son as the one the Father has chosen to be His bride.

So while you and I can rest assured of the heavenly Father's love for us, will we be a bride that is pleasing to His Son? We don't have to guess. We don't have to live in the fear that He might be disappointed in us. The Bible gives us enough information to know with certainty whether we will be pleasing to Him or not. While no one is perfect, it's possible for saved sinners to pursue lives of utter devotion, abandoned to the One who loves us and gave Himself for us—lives that reflect the beauty of His character in ways that are obvious to those around us.

In the following pages, Rachel-Ruth explores twenty-one qualities we find in Rebekah, each of which should be present in anyone who seeks to be pleasing to the Son. Please join us in this twenty-one-day challenge as we examine ourselves in preparation for meeting Jesus face-to-face. It's time to move our faith from salvation to transformation in order to be a bride who "has made herself ready."[65]

DAY 1

A Family Member

Before he had finished praying, Rebekah came out
with her jar on her shoulder. She was the daughter
of Bethuel son of Milcah, who was the wife of
Abraham's brother Nahor.

—Genesis 24:15

WHEN ABRAHAM INSTRUCTED HIS FAITHFUL SERVANT
to find a bride for his beloved son Isaac, he had
only one criterion: Make sure you find a young woman
who is in the family. His exact words were "Go to my
country and my own relatives and get a wife for my son
Isaac."[1] He didn't say to his servant, "Travel all the lands
in every kingdom, and find Isaac a wife that is drop-

dead gorgeous, wealthy, smart, athletic, the life of the party, and a really good cook!" While surely he would have wanted his son's bride to exhibit the qualities we've highlighted in this volume, the success of this mission was based first on her being a member of Abraham's extended family. Why was that so important?

God had promised to give the land of Canaan to Abraham and his descendants forever. However, during the time of Abraham, the land was occupied by Canaanites, a broad term used to describe ten tribes that lived in the land. The Canaanites were wicked people that worshipped idols, sacrificed children, and glorified every kind of sexual perversion, to name just a few of their sinful patterns. Abraham had the wisdom to know that Isaac needed a godly wife and that such a woman wouldn't be found among the pagan tribes surrounding them. So he sent his servant on a long trek back to Abraham's hometown of Haran, where his brother's family still lived.

Being a mother of three daughters, two of whom are at the age where they could meet their future spouses, I resonate with Abraham's concern. As you can imagine, each of my daughters has a very different vision of the type of man she hopes to one day marry. There has been much discussion and prayer in our house over what the man of their dreams will be like and look like. But the one thing I always say with absolute conviction is "Make sure he is in God's family!"

The primary qualification is that he has to love Jesus with all his heart and be surrendered to the Lord and His will for his life.

Beauty fades; financial prosperity can come and go; athletic records will be broken by the next star. But a marriage centered on a shared love for Jesus will endure whatever life may throw at you. So when one of my daughters calls to tell me she is going on a date, the first thing I ask is if he is a believer. In other words, Is he in God's family?

As I consider what it means to be in the family, I can't help but think of my dad, Danny Lotz. As a teenager, he was an aggressive, six-foot-seven basketball player who started all four years on the basketball team at Northport High School on Long Island, New York, and played pickup basketball in Harlem every chance he got. All that hard work paid off when he received a full basketball scholarship to the University of North Carolina. Tar Heel country! While playing under Coach Frank McGuire, my dad and his team had an undefeated season, winning the 1957 national championship in triple overtime against Kansas.

I obviously wasn't alive at that time, but growing up, I saw the many perks my dad enjoyed from being a part of the Tar Heel's basketball family: season tickets to athletic events, membership in the lettermen's club, camaraderie with all the former and current players and coaches, a fiftieth anniversary ring ceremony honoring their dream championship season, photos of their team on display in the Dean Dome, an entire museum dedicated to UNC basketball, and the list goes on. Wherever legendary UNC coach Dean Smith was, if he saw my dad, he would stop everything to go talk with him. Because when you are part of UNC basketball, you are part of an exclusive family! When longtime head coach Roy Williams announced his retirement in 2021, many former UNC players made it clear that the school needed to hire a new coach within "the family." They did!

As exclusive as the UNC basketball family is, or Abraham's family was, God's family is even more exclusive. Even so, anyone is welcome to join! It doesn't matter what you look like—your height, your weight, your skin color. It doesn't matter how many academic degrees you have or don't have, how many championships you've won or lost, how much money is in your bank account or if you're overdrawn, or whether the latest fashions are hanging in your closet or you can't remember when you had new clothes. It doesn't matter how many times you've helped an old lady across the street, stopped along the road to fix someone's tire, cooked a meal for a sick friend, or given time or money to a homeless shelter. None of these things matter, because it's not about good works or good looks. It's about your relationship with the Father.

When the trumpet sounds and the clouds part and Jesus Himself descends, the only people that will be taken up to meet Him in the air and forever live in His house are those who are members of His family! That is the picture God was painting when He had Abraham seek a bride for his son Isaac, mirroring His own search for a bride suitable for His Son.

Jesus isn't the kind of princely bridegroom you read about in novels or see in movies, the kind that slays the dragon or fights off a villain or two to win the heart of the lovely princess. Our Bridegroom—the Son of God—came to this earth in human form, humbled Himself to leave glorious Heaven and be born in a stable, grew up, compassionately healed the sick, set free the demon possessed, raised the dead, led the sinner out of the path of destruction, and taught the hardest of hearts about the love of His Father. He was then rejected by His own people.[2] They spit at Him, mocked Him, hurled insults at Him, whipped Him, beat Him, pulled out His beard, nailed Him to a cross, and speared His side. But Jesus, our Bridegroom, didn't storm off; He didn't yell back; He didn't command them all to drop dead; He didn't pour out His wrath on humanity right then and there. Instead, our Prince, our Bridegroom, received all the wrath and condemnation we deserved. He took our sins on Himself and bore the humiliation of the Cross so that we could be set free and become His bride!

Oh, how can we be deserving of such a gift, such a Bridegroom? That's just it: We aren't worthy in ourselves. But this is the greatest news anyone can ever tell you: Jesus did all the work on the cross, all that was necessary for us to receive forgiveness of sins—past, present, and future. To be in God's exclusive family, all we have to do is believe and humbly accept His gift! Once we do receive this through faith in Jesus, "to those who [have] believed in his name, he [gives] the right to become children of God."[3]

Before the dear servant set out on his journey, he asked Abraham what he should do if the woman he chose as the bride wasn't willing to come back to Canaan and marry Isaac. Abraham responded by saying that the servant would then be released from the promise he'd made to find a bride for Isaac.[4] In other words, he shouldn't force her to come with him. The servant could choose a wife for Isaac, but then the potential bride would also have to willingly choose to come to Isaac's home and be part of his family.

Abraham's servant is like the Holy Spirit, coming to you with the most amazing offer imaginable. He offers you salvation in the name of Jesus! Will you accept? He won't force you. You have free will to choose. Don't delay; accept His free gift of salvation today! Make sure you are part of God's family.

DAY 1 CHALLENGE

If you don't remember a time when you prayed a prayer like the one below, how do you know you are in God's family? So on this first day, if you aren't sure, pray this prayer now. Don't wait another second! The Bridegroom is at the door. He's coming in the blink of an eye. Make sure He's coming for you!

Jesus, I believe! I want to be a member of Your Father's family!

I believe that You died on the cross to forgive me of my sins and cleanse me. I believe that You rose from the dead and now offer me eternal life with You and that one day You will return as my Bridegroom and receive me into Your kingdom in Heaven. I confess to You that I have done wrong things, and I'm sorry. I'm willing to turn away from them. I'm asking that You come into my life today. I receive the eternal life You offer. Be my Savior, the Forgiver of all my sins, the Lord of my life, and my soon-coming Bridegroom!

Thank You, Jesus!
Amen.

If you have the blessed assurance that God is your Father because you have trusted Jesus as your Savior and Lord, then take a moment now to thank Him for your place in His family.

> *Father God,*
>
> *Thank You for the confidence I have that I have met the most important criterion for being chosen as a bride for Your Son, Jesus. Not because of anything I am or have done but simply because I have placed all my trust in Him, I know I'm a member of Your family. Now I pray You will use the following twenty days of challenges to make me more pleasing to You in every way.*
>
> *For the sake of the Bridegroom,*
> *And in His name—Jesus,*
> *Amen.*

DAY 2

Faithful in the Day-to-Day

Before he had finished praying, Rebekah came out
with her jar on her shoulder.

—Genesis 24:15

HAVE YOU EVER ENVISIONED THAT GLORIOUS DAY WHEN
Jesus will appear? Have you wondered about
what He will find you doing—or possibly catch you
doing? The Bible says that He will come suddenly, like
a thief in the night.[1] There will be no five-minute
warning. You won't be able to call a time-out to stop
the argument you're in the middle of, break off your
adulterous affair, get sober after you've had too much
to drink, change the conversation at your gossipy lun-

cheon, put your phone down and open the Bible, shift from angry words to joyful praise in traffic, or stay late and help your co-worker instead of rushing home after work.

His coming will be swift. What will He find you doing? My grandmother, whom we called Tai Tai, hung over her kitchen sink a sign that said "Divine Service Will Be Conducted Here Three Times Daily." It was a continual reminder that even mundane, everyday chores should be done as unto the Lord. The Bible confirms that cooking and cooking pots, traveling and transportation, as well as other mundane items for day-to-day activities will one day have "Holy to the Lord" inscribed on them.[2] So when I'm in the middle of cooking another dinner or driving to one more prac-tice or answering a never-ending stream of emails, I need to take a deep breath and remember that every-thing I do should be done as unto Him. For His glory.

As much as we might like to hide away and wait for His return, we can't. We must continue to faith-fully live for Jesus in the everyday, including life's not-so-glamorous tasks. However, in the middle of those menial tasks, we can have an incredible encounter with God.

When the servant first spotted Rebekah, in the early evening, she was carrying a jar on her shoulder to collect water from the well. She was busy about her daily responsibilities. She wasn't gossiping with friends or taking a nap or binge-watching Netflix. Never would she have dreamed that a servant of a very wealthy man was nearby, seeking a bride for his princely son, but because she was faithful to carry out her responsibilities for that day, she was noticed and approached by Abraham's servant.

Retrieving water in a jar seems like a job that would make you feel unnoticed or less than someone else. It seems like a task to hand off to others. I've certainly tried to do that with some of my tasks a time or two! But the opposite was true for Rebekah. She was noticed *because* she was faithfully doing her work, indicated by a water jar on her shoulder, even after a long day.

My dad's youngest brother, Uncle Denton, told me once that so much of the Christian's walk is just being faithful in the everyday ho-hum. And God can meet you in that daily ho-hum, not just at the Rapture.

We see several such encounters with God in Scripture. Moses encountered God when he was on the far side of the desert, tending his father-in-law's sheep. God spoke to him through a burning bush and called him to return to Egypt, where God would use him to set His people free from slavery.[3] Gideon encountered God while threshing wheat. He was a fearful, unconfident man, yet God called him "mighty warrior" and sent him to fight the Midianites and save Israel.[4] Peter encountered the Lord while fishing on a boat. Jesus called him to be a disciple and eventually to open the door for the gospel to go to the Gentiles.[5] The woman at the well encountered Jesus while filling her jar with water. Jesus, the Living Water, completely changed her life in one conversation![6] Mary and Martha opened their home and served a meal to others and had a front row seat to Jesus's ministry.[7]

Each of these men and women was faithfully carrying out their day-to-day tasks when they encountered God in a personal, life-changing way.

Could that be you? Are you, like them, faithfully working day in and day out? Whether you are a dentist drilling teeth, a janitor scrubbing toilets, a mom in the car-pool line waiting to pick up kids, a dad helping your son with math homework, an administrative assistant on the twenty-second floor of an urban high-rise, a butcher in the back of a tiny grocery store, a dog walker, a CEO in a meeting, or a cashier at a checkout line—whatever work the Lord has you doing—are you faithful, no matter how monotonous the work? God is watching you go the extra mile on a certain project. He sees that you don't cut corners to finish early, even though others do. He sees you completing an assignment instead of procrastinating. He even watches you stay up late to do the dishes, start a load of laundry, pack your kids' lunches. He sees you wake up early to pray and study the Bible before you leave for a busy day at work. God is watching, even when you think no one else sees or cares! God also knows just when to step in with a word of encouragement for you, give you clear leading toward a new direction, or open a door of opportunity!

In 2 Kings 3, we find a great example. King Joram of Israel was a wicked king, although not as wicked as his parents, King Ahab and Queen Jezebel. Knowing the Moabites were about to attack, King Joram recruited King Jehoshaphat of Judah, along with the king of Edom, to join him in fighting the Moabites. Things didn't go so well. After seven days of chasing the Moabites, the armies ran out of water. King Joram threw a tantrum. Godly King Jehoshaphat, by contrast, suggested they inquire of the Lord through the prophet Elisha. The prophet's response cracks me up. He told Joram that he wouldn't have looked at him or even noticed him, but because Jehoshaphat was present, he would call on the Lord for them!

God's solution to their thirst: Have the soldiers dig ditches! They were to spend all night filling the valley with ditches. Imagine how they must have been tempted to grumble. "Why do we have to dig ditches? Do we have to dig that many ditches? Surely He didn't mean the whole valley. We can probably just dig a couple little holes. What's the big deal?" But they obeyed and faithfully dug what I assume were hundreds of ditches in the valley without cutting corners. The next morning God supernaturally filled that dry valley with water for the soldiers and the livestock—without one raindrop! God took care of them, but He wanted to see that they would faithfully carry out the task He assigned.

All the signs of the times suggest we don't have a whole lot of time left until Jesus returns. What will He find you doing? What task has He assigned to you that you feel isn't very significant? Your work? Your chores at home? Are you stuck in a house caring for a sick loved one instead of out doing "real work"? Whatever it may be, God is watching! Wouldn't it be wonderful to hear Him exclaim, "Well done, good and faithful servant! You have been faithful with a few things; I will put you in charge of many things"?[8] So . . . be faithful in the day-to-day!

DAY 2 CHALLENGE

What are your daily responsibilities? Examine your attitude toward them. Are you complaining about the demands of life, or are you grateful for the opportunity to serve faithfully with all your strength? King Solomon, the wisest man who has ever lived other than Jesus, challenged the reader of his memoirs, "Whatever your hand finds to do, do it with all your might."[9] On this second day, as you prepare to see Jesus face-to-face, commit to ensuring that He will find you faithfully doing the work He has called you to do—with all your heart.

Lord of my days,

I worship You as the carpenter in Nazareth, fulfilling orders for customers, doing the bidding of Joseph. I am sorry when I complain about the day-to-day. Help me see You in my responsibilities, whether they are small or overwhelming. Lift up my eyes to see that even while I am "digging ditches," I can have an incredible encounter with You. In that split second of the Rapture, when the sky unfolds and You return for me and I see You face-to-face, I want to be found faithful!

For the sake of the Bridegroom,
And in His name—Jesus,
Amen.

DAY 3

Beautiful . . . on the Inside

The girl was very beautiful.

—Genesis 24:16

SINCE I WAS A YOUNG GIRL, I'VE STRUGGLED WITH insecurity about my appearance, never feeling like I quite measured up. I've been at war with my curly hair for as long as I can remember. On top of that, I grew to my full height of five feet eleven in eighth grade. I towered over everyone, which was great on the basketball court but not so great in the halls at school, where everyone else seemed half my height! To this day, I have to remind myself that so-called perfect hair and ideal height aren't what matter in life.

When it comes to true beauty, what really matters is the heart. Sadly, outward beauty seems an obsession for most people. Everyone wants to look a certain way, so they do whatever it takes and pay however much it costs in the hope of achieving that perfect look. As women, we can move quickly from highlights to concealers and eye creams, to teeth whiteners, serums, fake lashes, self-tanners, diets, exercise, fashion, and even surgeries. While women seem more obvious in their obsession with outward appearance, men also can get caught up in their appearance, using teeth whiteners, self-tanners, bodybuilding exercises, and trendy hairstyles and clothes—all to appear successful or earn that compliment or capture the perfect selfie, TikTok, or Instagram post!

With four women in our house, you can imagine how much time, energy, and money are spent on hair and makeup! I would be lying if I said I didn't notice or lament the signs of aging that seem to be creeping up on me. But what does it really matter? I have to keep reminding myself that when we stand before God, He won't be looking to determine if I am pretty enough or if you are handsome enough to come into His heavenly Home. He won't question if we looked sharp while we shared the gospel down on earth. He won't ask to see how many likes we got on a certain vacation post. Beauty that counts for eternity is on the inside.

Abraham's servant noticed that Rebekah was beautiful—an outward characteristic—but what convinced him she was Isaac's future bride was her character.

Perhaps you've encountered a physically beautiful person, only to find out that they have bad manners, a filthy mouth, a huge ego, a haughty heart, or are just plain mean. The allure of their beauty quickly fades with the revelation of their character. Proverbs 31:30–31 says, "Charm is deceptive, and beauty is fleeting; but a woman who fears the LORD is to be praised. Give her the reward she has earned, and let her works bring her praise at the city gate."

We need to be men and women of character so that, even in the toughest circumstances, in the most menial jobs, when we face life's hardest curveballs, our beauty goes deeper than the surface. Paul described this beauty as "the fruit of the Spirit" . . . the evidence of a Christlike life. It's love, joy, peace, patience, kindness, goodness, faithfulness, gentleness, and self-control.[1] As our story continues, we will see that it was not just outer beauty but inner beauty that Rebekah had.

The enemy of our souls has created such an overpowering obsession with outer beauty in our culture that people don't seem to be able to handle the emotional turmoil of not aligning with the world's standards of beauty. This kind of pressure leads many into a state of depression or even hopelessness. God never intended for our focus to be on the outer, but it is a war tactic of the Enemy to distract us from what really counts—Christlike character.

But the Enemy's strategy isn't a new one. In 1 Samuel 16, the prophet Samuel went looking for the man God had chosen to be the future king of Israel. God led him to the family of Jesse in Bethlehem, where he met Jesse's first son, Eliab. He must have been a very handsome warrior, because Samuel was immediately impressed by his looks and assumed that he must be God's anointed. But the Lord corrected Samuel and said, "Do not consider his appearance or his height, for I have rejected him. The Lord does not look at the things man looks at. Man looks at the outward appearance, but the Lord looks at the heart."[2] So Jesse had seven of his sons pass in front of Samuel. None of them were God's chosen king. When the prophet asked if Jesse had any other sons, he learned that the youngest son was out tending the sheep. David was then brought before Samuel, and the Lord told Samuel, "Rise and anoint him; he is the one."[3] Even though Scripture says that David was "ruddy, with a fine appearance and handsome features,"[4] what singled him out as God's chosen future king of Israel was his heart.

When one of my daughters was in elementary school, a classmate sent out invitations to her birthday party. On the day of the event, I dropped my daughter off at the girl's house. When I returned to pick her up, she got into the car in tears. She told me that one student in her class—a little girl with a disability—hadn't been invited. I don't know what reasoning lay behind the cruelty of not inviting the child, but my daughter and I were grieved at what the exclusion suggested. What are we teaching our children, even at a young age? The way someone looks— the color of their skin, their clothing, their physical inabilities, and other outward characteristics—should never determine how we treat them.

Beauty doesn't last, and it doesn't matter in the long run, unless you just want to be remembered as pretty. What a shallow life that would be! Consider the greats in the Bible. We don't know what most of them looked like, but we read about their character and godliness, and it's literally life changing! Paul worshipping God in a prison cell;[5] John getting a fresh vision of Jesus while in exile;[6] Stephen having peace on his face while being stoned to death;[7] Jeremiah being thrown into a pit for his unyielding stand for the Lord;[8] Hosea being faithful to a wife who was continually unfaithful to him.[9] Like Samuel, maybe you and I need to refocus on inner beauty—the beauty of a Christlike character, which draws people to us and ultimately to Jesus.

When we stand before God, we won't be digging for our new lipstick or fixing our hair or polishing our Jordans or flexing our biceps to impress God. Our character will be what is on full display. Make it a priority to be beautiful on the inside.

DAY 3 CHALLENGE

Pause now and consider: How much time do you spend on your outward appearance compared with the time you spend in daily prayer and Bible reading? Do you need to make an adjustment? On this third day, if it's your goal to be truly beautiful in God's eyes, make it a priority to develop your character by spending time with Him, then live out your faith so that others can see Him reflected in you.

Fairest Lord Jesus,

How could I ever desire anything other than to be a reflection of You? So polish me using whatever means You choose . . . stress or suffering . . . problems or persecution . . . obstacles or opportunities . . . hard work or hard times. I'm Yours to mold into a person who is beautiful in Your eyes.

For the sake of the Bridegroom,
And in His name—Jesus,
Amen.

DAY 4

Purified

> The girl was very beautiful, a virgin; no man had ever lain with her.
>
> —Genesis 24:16

RECENTLY MY YOUNGEST DAUGHTER, RIGGIN, WAS having lunch with a group of other fifteen-year-old girls when some of the girls began telling stories of their sexual encounters. Riggin was disturbed by the direction of the conversation and knew that she needed to speak up. She began telling them about purity and how she is going to save sex for marriage. They looked at her, confused. They never got angry with her or laughed at her. Instead, they peppered her with questions. The girls at the table acted as if they had never heard or thought of that before! In fact, one girl shared that her father told her that in high school she would do a lot of "things," which he said was fine as long as she didn't take any pills. *That breaks my heart!* Have we fallen so far that we aren't teaching our children about God's basic principles for life?

After lunch, one of the girls came up to Riggin and thanked her for telling them about purity. She truly seemed appreciative, but their conversation underscored the unfortunate reality that purity seems to be a foreign concept to the generations growing up in our world today. Is that because people don't care about sin? Or perhaps, like Riggin's friends, they just haven't heard or thought about it. Have they been taught that the goal of life is happiness, as if there were no right or wrong? The prevailing mentality seems to be just do anything and everything that makes you feel happy. Have sex with whomever, drink as much alcohol as you want, snort/smoke/inject anything that makes you feel good, lie if you think it will be beneficial, look at pornography, gossip, be mean, steal, cheat—you name it. All of this may feel good in the moment, but sin inevitably leaves people feeling dirty, angry, and even hopeless whether or not they admit it. This downward spiral puts them on a course to mask their feelings by doing more of the same or worse. Sin is eating people alive, and they don't know what to do about it. Many of them don't even know what it is.

Several years ago, one of my girls accidentally left a chocolate candy bar in the pocket of a shirt she placed in the laundry pile. When I pulled the laundry out of the washing machine, chocolate was melted and smeared all over her clothes and everything else that was in the same load of laundry. Like any good procrastinating mom, I threw the whole pile into a trash bag and determined to figure out how to get chocolate out of fifty different fabrics—later. When I finally researched how I could salvage the clothes, I read that a certain brand of dish soap could get rid of chocolate stains. I wet and scrubbed each piece of laundry with water and dish soap, and the stains began to lighten. But despite my best efforts, a yellow stain was left behind on each piece of clothing.

Sin in our lives is like those chocolate stains. It permeates our hearts, spreading a stain that taints our relationships and other aspects of life. We can ignore the sin, put off confessing it, or try to mask it through pills, alcohol, therapy, good deeds, frantic busyness, or many other things. But only Jesus can get the stain of sin out of our hearts. And unlike my dish soap solution, He guarantees that His blood will wash us clean![1]

We are all sinners. There is no sin that you or I have committed that Jesus doesn't know about. And there is no sin that He won't forgive. First John 1:8–10 says, "If we claim to be without sin, we deceive ourselves and the truth is not in us. If we confess our sins, he is faithful and just and will forgive us our sins and purify us from all unrighteousness. If we claim we have not sinned, we make him out to be a liar and his word has no place in our lives."

Sexual immorality is especially devastating to the human spirit. I recently listened as a capable, successful young man, who is a friend of my brother, shared his story. He had married a woman who truly loved him. Because of his sinful past, however, he didn't think he deserved her love. So in a bizarre, twisted way, he proved he wasn't worthy by going out and having an adulterous affair. The misery was more than he could take. He ended up confessing his sin to the Lord, then to his wife, both of whom forgave him. Although it had been years since that terrible time, he wept as he recounted his story. It was evident the scars of sin were still painful.

When you and I give our lives to Jesus and become part of God's family, we are forgiven of every sin we have ever committed or will ever commit. Yet as Jesus followers, we must daily come to the Lord and confess to Him whatever sins we have committed that day so we can maintain our close relationship with Him. Sin puts distance between the Lord and us, a distance that we sometimes feel as a spiritual coldness or deadness or misery,[2] a lack of love for Him,[3] or prayers that aren't answered.[4]

My mom always taught me to keep short accounts with the Lord. God wants us to tell Him what we did, even though He already knows. He purifies us when we acknowledge our sin before Him, admit we were wrong, humbly and truthfully tell Him we are sorry for it, and stop that sinful behavior. He cleanses us of guilt and shame, leaving us washed clean on the inside. And it feels so good to be purified!

DAY 4 CHALLENGE

It's time for an internal scrubbing! On this fourth day, spend
time cleaning up. Don't worry about what the Lord will think
of your confession. He already knows about your sin, so just
tell Him. He won't blame you for it. Jesus actually shed His
blood in order to cleanse you and remove the stain of guilt.
The apostle Paul encouraged the Corinthians, "Do you not
know that the wicked will not inherit the kingdom of God?
Do not be deceived: Neither the sexually immoral nor idola-
ters nor adulterers nor male prostitutes nor homosexual of-
fenders nor thieves nor the greedy nor drunkards nor
slanderers nor swindlers will inherit the kingdom of God.
And that is what some of you were. But you were washed,
you were sanctified, you were justified in the name of the
Lord Jesus Christ and by the Spirit of our God."[5] So talk to the
Lord about your sin, confess it, stop indulging in whatever it
is at present, and ask Him to heal your memories of the past.
Ask Him to wash you on the inside—then enjoy being clean!
And know that on the day when He appears and you see
Him face-to-face, He will make everything new, erasing even
the memories of those sins![6]

Holy Lord,

You are high and lifted up. You live forever. Your very name is Holy.

I acknowledge that I am not. I am a sinner. Yet You have promised that You will live with those who are contrite and lowly in spirit, to revive our hearts.[7] I am so sorry for all the wrong things I have done and am currently doing. I am sorry for all the wrong things I have said. I confess to You my _____ (fill in the blank). I am willing to turn away from my sin. I choose to put effort into being found "spotless, blameless and at peace" with You when I see You face-to-face.[8] Help me! "Let me hear joy and gladness. . . . Restore to me the joy of your salvation."[9] Thank You for Your blood, which cleanses me from every sin, large and small, past and present.[10]

For the sake of the Bridegroom,
And in His name—Jesus,
Amen.

Spiritually Filled

She went down to the spring, filled her jar and
came up again.

—Genesis 24:16

MOST OF US HAVE THE LUXURY OF FILLING A GLASS
with water at the turn of a knob or the push of a
button. But Rebekah and the people of her day had to
retrieve their water from a well or a stream—a time-
consuming and muscle-straining daily chore, usually
reserved for women. After carrying a large empty jar on
her head or shoulder to wherever the well was located,
a woman would lower the jar into the well with a rope,
then pull the full—and heavy—jar to the top of the

well and carry the vessel back to her home for cooking, cleaning, and washing. Other wells were accessed by winding steps that descended into a recessed pool. A woman would walk down to dip her jar in the water, then walk back up the steps, lugging her heavy water-filled container.

While we don't know which type of well Rebekah accessed, either one would have required enormous effort in order for her to retrieve water. But for her to leave her family without water, for even a single day, would have been unthinkable. God has made water essential to human survival.

When my middle daughter, Sophia, was twenty months old, my husband, my two daughters (my youngest daughter had yet to be born), and I all got sick with the norovirus within thirty minutes of one another. It was quite a doozy. Neither of my girls was able to make it to the bathroom fast enough, so you can imagine. I've never done so much laundry in my life. We recovered after a week, but then Sophia caught it again. Unable to hold anything down, she became extremely weak and severely dehydrated. I called the nurse multiple times and was given the usual protocol: Wait fifteen minutes, and then give her a piece of ice to suck on. This went on for a while, but her precious little body still couldn't keep down the melted ice cube. She was becoming dangerously dehydrated, and

I was starting to panic! I felt helpless in my attempts to get the nurse to understand the seriousness of the situation.

In the middle of my agony, my mom asked if I had read *Daily Light,* a 365-day devotional that everyone in my family reads each morning. Because of our emergency situation, I hadn't read it that day. When I opened it and read the morning's portion, I cried. It's as if God spoke directly to me! He gave me a promise to claim for Sophia: "I, the LORD, keep it, I water it every moment; lest any hurt it, I keep it night and day."[1] I knew right then and there that God was promising me that He would "water" my little girl! The nurse finally was able to get us a room at the hospital, so I raced there in the pouring rain while Sophia lay limp in her car seat. I carried her down the hallway of the hospital to the room, where they made multiple attempts to get an IV into her tiny vein. And then . . . it worked! Fluid began dripping into her body, and she moved, opening her eyes. God saved her little life! With every drop of fluid that went into her small body, He gave me increasing peace.

Just as Sophia needed that IV fluid to live, just as each of us needs water to sustain life, we also need God's Word to replenish us so that we don't dry up. God confirmed the necessity of being spiritually filled when He explained, "As the rain and the snow come down from heaven, and do not return to it without watering the earth and making it bud and flourish, so that it yields seed for the sower and bread for the eater, so is my word that goes out from my mouth."[2]

We need to be aware of warning signs that we are spiritually dehydrated or in danger of slipping into that state. I've recently been reminded of how vital it is for me to stay filled with God's life-giving Word. Our family has been under enormous attack from the Enemy over the past year, especially during the past six months—an all-out aggressive assault with the intent to steal, kill, and destroy our faith. After illnesses, heartbreaking news, shattered dreams, intense confrontations, and near-death experiences, we've been left almost stunned. I personally had to deal with two rare SCAD (spontaneous coronary artery dissection) heart attacks that almost took my life, only to find out there is a chance I can have another one!

While writing this, I'm still having some chest pain, two months after my heart attacks. Several scares have sent me to the ER and to the doctor's office. But God has been giving me multiple promises through His Word that I will be okay, that I won't die from this! Recently I was praying about whether or not to go to the ER because of intense chest pain. God clearly spoke to me through Psalm 40, telling me to wait patiently and stand firm. So I chose to wait and not be fearful! Instead of going to the ER, I went to bed. When I woke up the next morning, the pain had greatly decreased. I knew God was testing my faith! That same week, as I ate dinner, I started to feel dizzy and my mouth, tongue, and chin started to tingle and grow slightly numb. I thought, *Could this really be happening? Heart problems and now an allergic reaction to some food?* What a week! I felt I was at the end of my rope. So I turned to God's Word. Psalm 46:10 seemed to jump off the page: "Be still, and know that I am God." I chose to sit still, not panic, and trust that God wouldn't allow it to get worse. The numbness and dizziness went away! While writing this, I was seeking God's will on whether or not it would be safe to leave town for the weekend for a meeting. I prayed, and God gave me a verse of confirmation in my devotions: "The LORD will keep you from all harm—he will watch over your life; the LORD will watch over your coming and going both now and forevermore."[3] I believe He clearly confirmed to me that I would be safe going on the trip! If I had chosen not to seek Him in each of the above situations, I would have been overtaken by fear.

God's Word fills me up to overflowing with living water: promises, encouragement, direction, and correction! God wants to be intimately involved in my life and yours. So when you face questions and problems and you need wisdom on what to do or what to say or where to go, turn to God's Word! Not only will it speak to you, but most important, it will keep your focus on Jesus and not your circumstances. Isn't it time you drank deeply of the Living Water?

DAY 5 CHALLENGE

What words are saturating your heart and mind? Are you filling up on words from the news, social media, movies, friends? Or are you drinking in the Word of God until it overflows in your thoughts, in your words, and in your life? On this day, commit to opening your Bible every day and read it, meditate on it, obey it, and let it transform your life! Don't dry up. Drink up instead. Stay spiritually filled!

Dear Jesus,

I have been restless within. Dissatisfied. Longing for something yet not knowing what. Seeking fulfillment in things that don't satisfy. But now I do know what's missing. I am thirsty for You. I am humbly asking You to give me a drink of the Living Water, which is Yourself.[4] You have given me this invitation: "Whoever is thirsty, let him come; and whoever wishes, let him take the free gift of the water of life."[5]

So right now, on day 5, as I open my Bible to read, please let me hear the whisper of Your Spirit speaking to me. Bring the verses to life. I ask You to fill me with Yourself through Your Word until I overflow. To the praise of Your glory.

For the sake of the Bridegroom,
And in His name—Jesus,
Amen.

DAY 6

Kind

The servant hurried to meet her and said, "Please give me a little water from your jar."

"Drink, my lord," she said, and quickly lowered the jar to her hands and gave him a drink.

—Genesis 24:17–18

NOTICING THE SERVANT'S DUSTY CLOTHING, THE weariness in his creased face, and his camels lined up by the well, Rebekah must have concluded he had traveled a long distance. When he asked for a drink, she didn't hesitate. Remarkably, she showed tremendous kindness to a perfect stranger. She lowered her jar and gave it to him. The water that had cost her time and energy to retrieve for herself and her own needs, Rebekah willingly, without hesitation, gave to him.

As those the Father has chosen to be the bride of His Son, we are exhorted to do the same: "As God's chosen people, holy and dearly loved, clothe yourselves with compassion, kindness, humility, gentleness and patience."[1] When we show kindness to someone, it's as if we are showing kindness to God Himself!

Yet that doesn't mean kindness is always the easy choice. Words fail to fully describe the amount of discord and hostility that permeate our world. Whether you are watching the news, walking through the grocery store, reading comments on Twitter or other social media, talking with friends or relatives, interacting with a teacher, watching a sporting event, or even ordering food at a restaurant, you hear and sometimes receive unkind words, looks, and gestures. These unfortunate interactions can start a chain reaction of hostility. We get hurt, turn around, and lash out at the next person in our path, and then they get hurt, turn around, and hurt the next person coming along. This cycle too often continues uninterrupted, leaving us exhausted, heavyhearted, and irritable.

God warned us that it would get worse in the last days before Jesus returns: "Mark this: There will be terrible times in the last days. People will be lovers of themselves, lovers of money, boastful, proud, abusive, disobedient to their parents, ungrateful, unholy, without love, unforgiving, slanderous, without self-control, brutal, not lovers of the good, treacherous, rash, conceited, lovers of pleasure rather than lovers of God—having a form of godliness but denying its power."[2]

Every description in those verses rings true today! So how do we respond? The easy response—and our natural, fleshly inclination—is to retaliate, to meet unkindness with unkindness instead of holding our tongues, to look out for ourselves instead of showing concern for others. We respond harshly to a spouse who hurt our feelings. We stick to our schedule rather than stopping to help someone in need. Or perhaps we refrain from being actively unkind to someone, but what do we say behind their back? So many times each day, we face a choice either to be kind or to respond in one of the negative ways described in those verses.

In these last days, the Enemy is on a mission to discourage and defeat us as never before. He can do it in subtle ways, causing little irritations that wear us down until we are short-tempered, impatient, and unkind. While writing this, I feel the Holy Spirit convicting me of a pattern of unkindness toward someone who has hurt me deeply in the past. Somehow in my mind, I've justified my lack of warmth because of the deep wounds I've suffered. I've told the Lord multiple times, "She doesn't deserve it." But I've also told Him I'm sorry and I've asked Him to please help me be kind to those who I sometimes feel deserve a good smack! I'm convicted about my less-than-kind perspective as I consider how, in *His* kindness, Jesus saved me by His grace, redeemed me by His own blood, and will one day return to take me to His heavenly Home. That's kindness I know I don't deserve, but I want to "pay it forward" as I wait for that great day!

You and I must be diligent in our efforts to be kind in every encounter we have throughout our day and be quick to correct ourselves and set it right when we fail. It takes enormous effort, humility, and self-control to be kind in a world full of aggressive and hostile people.

Why be kind? The simple answer: Because God said so. Ephesians 4:31–32 says, "Get rid of all bitterness, rage and anger, brawling and slander, along with every form of malice. Be kind and compassionate to one another, forgiving each other, just as in Christ God forgave you."

Our kindness should overflow no matter our circumstances, no matter how we are treated, and no matter how we are feeling. Jesus showed kindness and compassion to the sick, to the hurting, and to those who were shunned by everyone else, even when He was tired and hungry.

You may have heard of Corrie ten Boom, who, along with her sister Betsie, was arrested for hiding Jews during the Nazi occupation of the Netherlands. When they were taken to the Ravensbrück concentration camp, Corrie was able to smuggle in a small bottle of vitamin drops. Knowing that she and Betsie would be malnourished from the small "meals" they were given by the guards, they put a drop of vitamins on their piece of bread each day. Other women around them were sick too, so out of kindness they shared the drops, even though they knew that their small bottle wouldn't last long. More and more women came for drops, yet the bottle never ran out! God supernaturally supplied vitamin drops for everyone as long as needed.[3] What do I learn from that story? I should never selfishly withhold kindness and compassion from others, even if it looks like I will lose out.

As things deteriorate around the world economically and in other ways, we will have more and more opportunities to share God's kindness with those around us. Has God blessed you with finances? Give. Do you know someone who is sick? Make a meal for them. Is someone you know in tough circumstances? Send them an encouraging text, or offer the gift of your time. Have you been yelled at by a boss, co-worker, or family member? Respond with patience, and look for a way you can bless them. Be kind!

DAY 6 CHALLENGE

Carefully consider your interactions each day, with your family and friends, with your co-workers, with your neighbors, with the checkout cashier, and with your fellow drivers. How can you show kindness to each person? On this day, identify a specific situation in which you can serve someone else with kindness, especially someone who has not been kind to you. Then do it!

Tender Lord,

How I praise You for Your loving-kindness. So many times when I have been discouraged or defeated, You have intervened by moving someone to reach out to me with an encouraging word.[4] Thank You. In gratitude for Your kindness to me, I want to show kindness to others. Please prompt me to encourage others by my kind words and deeds, regardless of the way they treat me, until it becomes a habit.[5]

For the sake of the Bridegroom,
And in His name—Jesus,
Amen.

A Humble Servant

After she had given him a drink, she said, "I'll draw water for your camels too, until they have finished drinking."

—Genesis 24:19

WE LIVE IN A NARCISSISTIC WORLD WHERE SERVING someone else without expectation of reward is viewed as ludicrous. The prevailing philosophy is "Whatever benefits me and makes me happy takes precedence over everything else." And how many of us proudly refuse to serve because it's "not my job"?

Rebekah's behavior offers a starkly different picture of how we are to live as followers of Jesus, especially as the end draws near. We know from yesterday's challenge that Rebekah showed kindness to a total stranger by giving him water from her jar, which she had just filled from the well. She could have walked away feeling good about herself and her kind gesture. But what she did next blows my mind!

As she watched this thirsty old servant drink from her jar, she noticed his ten camels looking dusty and thirsty as well. She could have told the servant and his men to help themselves to the water in the well and to have a nice journey. No one would have viewed her as anything less than a kind and mannerly young lady. But instead, after giving the servant a drink, she offered to water *all* his camels too. How astounding! Unlike a dog or a cat, a camel isn't satisfied with a single bowlful of water. After a long, hot journey, a camel will drink up to thirty gallons of water in ten minutes.[1] Rebekah very well may have retrieved three hundred gallons of water for the camels! Can you imagine the amount of backbreaking work that would have required? And she hadn't been ordered to do it. It wasn't even expected of her. And it certainly wasn't her job. She was the daughter of a privileged family. Yet she willingly chose to serve. That takes humility.

Abraham's servant had specifically prayed, "May it be that when I say to a girl, 'Please let down your jar that I may have a drink,' and she says, 'Drink, and I'll water your camels too'—let her be the one you have chosen for your servant Isaac."[2] He wanted a way to identify God's choice for Isaac out of all the girls that would be coming to the well. By asking God to show him in this way, he would also learn much about her character. Rebekah served selflessly and humbly without regard for her own time and energy, with no expectation of reward. It's hard to imagine anyone doing that. Yet as Jesus followers, shouldn't we be known for that kind of willingness to serve?

Consider what Jesus told His disciples: "If anyone wants to be first, he must be the very last, and the servant of all."[3] I don't know about you, but I struggle to live this out consistently. I strive but fall short so many times. I often come to the end of the day and realize there were many moments when I could have served even in the simplest ways and yet I didn't. I could have warmed up my husband's meal when he came home from work late, instead of letting him get it himself. I could have folded my daughter's clean clothes instead of leaving them in a pile for her to fold when she came in exhausted after practice. As I reflect on this day's challenge, I desire to serve my family with a more willing spirit as well as try to anticipate people's needs and better serve them.

My brother, Jonathan, has been a great example to me. Since my heart attacks, he's come to my house on multiple occasions to sit with me so I wouldn't be alone in case I had another emergency, or just to keep me company. Sometimes he'll show up with lunch or a chai latte without me even asking for it.

I remember one day I just couldn't seem to get warm. I got up to get something, and when I came back, he was standing in front of the fireplace, holding my blanket up so that the fire would warm it! When I sat down, he brought it over to me and laid it on my lap. I was in tears at his thoughtfulness.

He's plunged my toilets, scrubbed my floors, changed my lightbulbs, and even brought a weather strip for my drafty front door and applied it without being asked. I've never met anyone who enjoys serving more than Jonathan and who does it with such humility. There is never a job too big or too menial for him. Many times I've been with him in fast food restaurants, or walking down a sidewalk, or in a store, and I'll step over a tissue or a napkin someone has dropped without giving it a second thought. But Jonathan always bends down, picks it up, and throws it away, regardless of how dirty the piece of trash might be. He wipes restaurant tables down with hand sanitizer so we can enjoy a clean space. He continually looks for ways he can serve others, including strangers.

As we were growing up, my dad repeatedly emphasized that our lives are never about us. We need to be others-focused. He frequently quoted Matthew 20:28: "The Son of Man did not come to be served, but to serve." Jesus—who created the universe, put the planets in place, knows all the stars by name, created every cell in our complex bodies, knows our every thought before we think it, determines the times and the seasons—He is higher than any ruler or principality. Yet this divine, all-powerful King got on His knees and washed His disciples' dirty, grimy, stinky feet! Can you imagine the discomfort, even dismay, of the disciples as they submitted to His washing their feet, knowing they should have been washing His? Jesus told them, "I have set you an example that you should do as I have done for you."[4] How can any of us think we are too educated, too important, too clean, too above serving, if that's what Jesus did? We are to value others above ourselves, having the same mindset as Christ Jesus.[5]

In Matthew 24:45–46, Jesus said to His disciples, "Who then is the faithful and wise servant, whom the master has put in charge of the servants in his household to give them their food at the proper time? It will be good for that servant whose master finds him doing so when he returns." Jesus is the Master who is coming! When He returns, will He find you doing whatever needs to be done, regardless of your position or what the task is? Be a humble servant.

DAY 7 CHALLENGE

If someone were to ask your friends, family, co-workers, or neighbors how often you serve them in some way, what would their answer be? On this day, ask God to show you what you can do today to serve those around you. Then, regardless of the time and cost to yourself, do it. For Jesus's sake.

Son of Man,

You are also the Son of God, who was seated on the throne of glory, yet You made Yourself nothing, taking the very nature of a servant, being made in human likeness. As a result, God has exalted You to the highest place.[6] *You are even now seated at His right hand with all things placed under Your feet.*[7]

I confess my pride when I consider some tasks beneath me, some people too small to help, or some deed not significant enough for my time. Teach me that the way up is down. I choose to serve others as I would serve You.

For the sake of the Bridegroom,
And in His name—Jesus,
Amen.

DAY 8

Responsive to Needs

She quickly emptied her jar into the trough, ran back to the well to draw more water, and drew enough for all his camels.

—Genesis 24:20

EVEN THOUGH IT WAS YEARS AGO, I STILL REMEMBER clearly what it was like being desert-mouthed thirsty at basketball practice in high school. We didn't get frequent water breaks like athletes do nowadays. My coach would run us into the ground before she'd finally blow the whistle and let us get water. This was before water bottles, and no one brought water jugs from home. We had to use the good old-fashioned water fountain, which dribbled out a tiny stream you could catch only with your mouth millimeters away from touching the drain. Disgusting. But we didn't care. When the whistle blew, every player shifted to an all-out sprint to try to get to the water fountain first. Without fail, someone took a long time drinking while everyone yelled at her. "Move!" "Let someone else have a turn!" "Stop hogging the fountain!" Then the coach would blow the whistle to signal that practice was about to restart. The last three or so girls would literally get one squirt of water and have to race back into the gym, thirst not even remotely quenched!

The camels in our story couldn't go fight in line like my basketball team. Nor could they grab a bucket, lower it into the well, pull it back up, and proceed to gulp water. First of all, camels don't have hands. And second—well, the whole scenario is ludicrous. The point is, someone had to bring the water to the camels. They needed Rebekah! She answered their clear signs of thirst with water from the well. She didn't put it off to a more convenient time. The camels would have shriveled up and died. Instead, she ran quickly to the well to draw more water and give it to them. The long journey in the desert heat didn't consume the camels, because she immediately responded to their need for water.

We live in a world of people who, like those camels, are dying of thirst, drying up in a desert that offers only a mirage of false satisfaction. They are attempting to quench their thirst through food, social media, sex, drugs, alcohol, friends, money, fame, influence, career, shopping, vacations, experiences, activism, trying out different religions, or blending a mix of beliefs to suit their preferences. Inevitably they discover that none of it satisfies long-term. Nothing quenches the thirst of their souls.

People all around us are empty and hopeless. The world is on a fast track to destruction, the end is drawing near, Jesus is coming—and we are the world's Rebekah! As believers, you and I have the life-giving water they need. We are the vessels that contain and overflow with the Living Water—Jesus![1] But how responsive are we to the need of these thirsty people?

A wonderful story in John's gospel describes Jesus walking through the narrow streets of Jerusalem, which were crowded with pilgrims who had come for one of the Jewish feasts. As He and His disciples walked past the Pool of Bethesda, they saw that it was mobbed by a great group of disabled people. Among them was a man who had been an invalid for thirty-eight years. John wrote, "When Jesus saw him lying there . . ."[2] Think of that for a moment! With thousands of people thronging the streets and hundreds pressed around the pool, how was it that Jesus noticed this one man? Somehow the man's desperate need, even though unspoken, must have arrested our Lord's attention. Jesus questioned the man and gave him instructions, which the man obeyed. The result? The man was healed! His life was radically transformed! All because Jesus had been responsive to the man's need.

During this past year my family has seen what can happen when we aim to follow His example.

A fellow student caught the attention of my fifteen-year-old daughter, Riggin, during the first weeks of school. It was evident he knew nothing about the Lord, had already made some really bad choices, and was basically raising himself. (This is more common than you might imagine as parents increasingly live for themselves.) One night over FaceTime, Riggin sensed his need. She began telling him that Jesus loved him and offered him forgiveness. He couldn't believe it! He was floored to discover that God wasn't angry with him but actually loved him. After a long conversation, Riggin asked if he wanted to give his life to Jesus. He said yes! She led him through the prayer of salvation. I was downstairs at the time, and although Riggin was on the phone upstairs, I could hear him shouting with excitement!

Not long ago, my middle daughter, Sophia, had dinner with a friend. Before the meal was served, she asked God's blessing. Later, the girl mentioned that she had never felt more peace in her life than when

Sophia prayed. Sophia recognized the young woman's need for Jesus and responded by sharing the gospel with her. Even though the girl had been raised in a religious home, she didn't know much about the Lord. So Sophia, responding to the girl's obvious need for inner peace through a personal relationship with Jesus, asked if she wanted to give her life to Jesus. She eagerly agreed! She was radically transformed and filled with His peace, and she immediately began growing in her new life with Jesus.

My mom, my sister Morrow, and I traveled to Arizona for some meetings. Upon leaving, as we headed to the airport, we struck up a conversation with our driver. All three of us sensed he had some things heavy on his heart. We could hear the pain in his voice. My mom responded by telling him about the love of Jesus. When we arrived at the airport and he pulled the car to the curb, my mom asked if he wanted to give his life to Jesus, be forgiven of his sins, and have the assurance that Heaven was his Home. He said yes! Then he prayed the prayer of salvation, phrase by phrase, after my mom, right there in the driver's seat—as he was still looking for a place to park. When we got out of the car, his expression, which had been unfriendly and remote when he picked us up, was now filled with light and joy!

All around us are people who need the Lord. But

we don't always have the opportunity to pray with them. A few days ago, my mom was having lunch with a friend. The server had a very humorous smile the entire time he waited on them. When Mom went to pay the bill, thinking he might be a believer whose joy was on his face, she asked if he knew Jesus. He said in a startled voice, "Who?" She responded, "Jesus. The Son of God. The One who died for you." The humor left his face, and he said he used to go to church a lot but hadn't been for years. Mom responded by telling him God had put her at his table to remind him that God loved him, and then she shared the gospel. She made it clear that Jesus had died for him not to get him into church or a religion but to invite him into a personal relationship. The mask that had been on the server's face dropped as he sincerely thanked Mom, saying he needed to hear that. Then he asked Mom, before walking away, to please come back and ask for his table. She continues to pray for him by name.

Who in your life is in need? Your server at a restaurant? Your classmate in school? Your neighbor down the street? Your co-worker in the next cubicle? There is literally no time to waste! The clock is ticking in this final hour. When we know we have the Living Water and people are dying of thirst, we must, like Rebekah, be responsive to their need.

DAY 8 CHALLENGE

When have you sensed someone's need for peace? Forgiveness? Hope? Love? Did you recognize that it was really a need for Jesus? How did you respond? On this day, ask God to make you aware of the needs of others; then ask Him to help you as you respond. Don't be intimidated. Don't be shy. Say His name. Commit to sharing God's love while there is still time. Don't make it confusing or difficult. Just speak sincerely, compassionately, from your heart, and let the fountain of His love flow out of you to quench the thirst of those around you!

Beloved Need Meeter,

You know all things. You know I need You, and therefore, I have You. You have given me strength, hope, peace, wisdom, joy, forgiveness, love, and the list goes on. I could not live without You!

Forgive me when I keep You to myself while there are people all around me who need You too. Give me a sharpened focus so that I look beyond myself. Give me eyes to see the one person in the crowd who has a desperate, unspoken need. Then prompt me to respond by just giving them Jesus.

For the sake of the Bridegroom,
And in His name—Jesus,
Amen.

DAY 9

Honest

Without saying a word, the man watched her
closely to learn whether or not the LORD had
made his journey successful.

—Genesis 24:21

REBEKAH HAD NO IDEA WHY THE MAN WAS THERE,
and I'm sure it never crossed her mind that she
was the actual focus of his long trek. She faithfully
watered all the camels, not realizing she was being
tested to see if she would finish the job. Abraham's
servant observed her as she went back and forth from
the well to the watering trough multiple times. Maybe
she was thinking about the other chores she needed to

get done before nightfall; maybe she was reflecting on a conversation she'd had earlier in the day with a friend; maybe she was wondering where the caravan of men had come from and where they were going. Whatever was on her mind, she did what she'd said she would do. She completed her work without becoming distracted, cutting corners, or giving up when she grew weary.

Such integrity is far too rare a trait in our society today. America and our world are plummeting further and further away from God's principles for living. Yesterday's headlines pale in comparison with today's. Accusations abound regarding fraudulent elections, bribes between governments, underhanded dealings between government officials and corporations, lies propagated in the media, and personal and political agendas prioritized over the public good, at the cost of truth. Hollywood movies glorify any form of cheating, including adultery. Websites offer old tests to facilitate cheating in school. The younger generations think nothing of lying to their friends, teachers, and parents. It seems to be as natural to them as drinking coffee.

God warned us that as the end draws near, the "birth pains" that include lawlessness will increase.[1] We are seeing that play out right before our eyes!

This is the time to showcase Christlike characteristics to a world crumbling under the weight of the obsession with getting our own way at any cost. Integrity shines all the more brightly—and unexpectedly—in the darkness of our self-serving, self-promoting, self-absorbed culture. I'm reminded of when the apostle Paul sent an offering to the church in Jerusalem and intentionally sent respected men with it, explaining, "We are taking pains to do what is right, not only in the eyes of the Lord but also in the eyes of men."[2] Our goal, too, should be to act with unimpeachable honesty and integrity.

Years ago, my cousin Will Graham, who is my age, was living with my parents while attending seminary nearby. He and my dad were hilarious together. They would pull pranks on each other, leave funny voice-mails, and just generally enjoy their shared sense of humor. They are two of the funniest people I know! One day Will called me about an assignment that was coming due. He asked if I had an old paper from college that he could copy and use for his ethics class. I about fell out of my chair! I laugh about that to this day. Even though Will was totally joking, the story makes a great point: As believers, we must have integrity in all we do, whether or not we're taking an ethics class!

One of my favorite Old Testament characters is Daniel. He was enslaved by King Nebuchadnezzar and lived in Babylon, where he rose to the heights of leadership under four world emperors. The third ruler he served was Darius, king of the Medes and Persians. Darius made plans to elevate Daniel to one of the highest leadership positions in his kingdom. The other administrators became jealous and sought to find grounds to bring charges against him in order to prevent the promotion. The biblical account records, "They could find no corruption in him, because he was trustworthy and neither corrupt nor negligent. Finally these men said, 'We will never find any basis for charges against this man Daniel unless it has something to do with the law of his God.'"[3] Daniel's integrity was recognized even by his enemies! In the end, his enemies tricked the king, arrested Daniel for praying, and had him thrown into the lions' den. But God honors those who honor Him. He shut the mouths of the lions, Daniel was rescued, God was glorified, and the accusers were then thrown into the lions' den themselves.

If, like Daniel's, your life were to be thoroughly investigated by your enemies, what would be revealed? What does integrity look like for you and me? When you are with your spouse and you receive a text, you tell your spouse who texted so there is no room for speculation. When you are filing your taxes, you enter everything without cheating. When you get a test back and realize your teacher marked "correct" on an answer that was actually wrong, you tell her. When the whole office is clocking incorrect hours and they ask you to do the same so no one gets caught, you don't, even if they get angry. When you've made a horrible mistake and the person you've wronged asks about it, you own up to it and repent. When your coach asks you how many shots you made during the drill, you tell him the correct number with no exaggeration. When you are a married person and a co-worker of the opposite sex asks you to eat lunch together, you don't because you want to avoid the appearance of evil and the temptation that it could lead to. When you tell your parents you are going to a friend's house to study, you go to the friend's house and study, not sneak out to a party.

A person of integrity should be an open book, never leaving room for doubt about their trustworthiness. A person of integrity doesn't cheat in any way, even if it will benefit them, even if they believe they'll never be caught. A person of integrity keeps their word, even when it isn't convenient. A person of integrity is someone you can count on. A person of integrity lets their yes be yes and their no be no. A person of integrity is always honest. A person of integrity is someone you want to be around and someone you want to be!

Jesus is coming back! In John's eyewitness account of the events leading up to and including the return of

Jesus, he testified that he saw Jesus with "eyes . . . like blazing fire."[4] Jesus sees right through you and me. We can't deceive Him. Or work around Him. Or fudge in our service to Him. Let His eyes have a purifying effect on what you say and what you do. Be transparent. Be honest.

DAY 9 CHALLENGE

Make a list of the promises and commitments you have made. Can your spouse, your children, your boss, trust you to do what you have said you will do? Do you finish what you start, without making excuses? On this day, ask God to reveal to you the areas of your work, actions, and speech where you have compromised or tolerated a lower standard of honesty. Tell God you are sorry. Then keep your promises, fulfill your commitments, and finish what you have started.

Son of David,

"You know me. You know when I sit and when I rise; you perceive my thoughts from afar. You discern my going out and my lying down; you are familiar with all my ways. Before a word is on my tongue you know it completely, O LORD. *. . . . Search me, O God, and know my heart; test me and know my anxious thoughts. See if there is any offensive way in me, and lead me in the way everlasting."*[5]

For the sake of the Bridegroom,
And in His name—Jesus,
Amen.

~~~~

Motivated

Without saying a word, the man watched her
closely. . . . When the camels had finished drinking, the man took out a gold nose ring weighing a
beka and two gold bracelets weighing ten shekels.

—Genesis 24:21–22

WE ALL FACE VARIOUS TRIALS AND DIFFICULTIES.
Sometimes they hit hard and fast; other times
they park and set up shop.

What are you dealing with right now? Do you have
a strenuous workload that leaves you exhausted beyond reason? Are you studying long hours in college
while also working a job? Are you suffering through

your third round of chemotherapy? Do you have a child whom you've trained and taught to love the Lord that is now living in total rebellion? Do you have bills to pay with no money in your bank account? Are you living in the agony of a loveless marriage? Have you just lost another baby to miscarriage? Are you dealing with a chronic illness that keeps you up at night? Whatever difficulty you are dealing with, the story of Rebekah reminds us of the immeasurable blessings that God has in store for us if we hold fast to our faith and glorify Him through whatever we endure.

Rebekah had just completed backbreaking work, drawing as much as three hundred gallons of water for ten thirsty camels, without any modern-day technology or conveniences! She didn't have a cushiony pair of Nikes to wear. Her feet must have been aching and even blistered, her shoulder muscles must have had a million knots in them, and her back must have throbbed. But all we know for certain is that she completed the task out of the goodness of her heart for a total stranger— and that the entire time she was engaged in this hard and hot labor, the man was watching.

And when her work was completed, the stranger gave her beautiful gold jewelry worth a small fortune. I doubt Rebekah expected a reward for her work, much less such extravagance! It was clearly not her motivation in helping.

Rebekah's story serves as a reminder of the reward that awaits you and me as the bride of Christ. As we work hard to faithfully discharge our responsibilities, as we sacrificially help others, as we endure trials or suffer in any way—God is watching us. And the Bible says that He will reward us! "Whatever you do, work at it with all your heart, as working for the Lord, not for men, since you know that you will receive an inheritance from the Lord as a reward. It is the Lord Christ you are serving."[1] Lest we lose sight of our reward, at the end of the Bible, Jesus reminds us, "Behold, I am coming soon! My reward is with me, and I will give to everyone according to what he has done."[2]

God sees all that you are going through, even when you think no one else does. He sees when you are passed up for a promotion and when you work hard as a volunteer. He sees the suffering you've experienced physically, mentally, or emotionally, and He knows that you still follow Him with your whole heart. He watches you stay up late caring for a sick child or an elderly parent. He sees you serve others with joy while silently grimacing in chronic pain. Whatever it is, God the Holy Spirit sees! He knows how to reward you far beyond your wildest imagination.

As I mentioned earlier, my dad played for the University of North Carolina Tar Heels basketball team. His sophomore year, his undefeated team topped off the season by beating Kansas and Wilt Chamberlain in triple overtime for the NCAA national championship. My dad was thrilled! He helped cut down the net, held up the winning trophy he had worked so hard to earn, and celebrated with his team that night. But, he told me years later, the next morning he felt somewhat empty. The thought that kept nagging at him was, *Is that all there is?* A moment. A memory. And a trophy that tarnished in the glass case of the university museum. The reward didn't seem to match a lifetime of practice, training, and sacrifice.

We can't possibly fathom how perfect and how great our eternal reward will be for our service to our Lord here. There will be no disappointment, no "is that all there is?" questions, when we get to Heaven. While we certainly don't serve the Lord just to get a reward, He knows our deeds and will give to each of us according to what we have done.[3]

Some of the rewards He promises will be given to those who are persecuted for His name's sake,[4] to those who love the unloving,[5] to those who give to the needy without showy pretense,[6] to those who pray and fast,[7] to those who give a cup of cold water to the thirsty.[8] The rewards are endless. Some are given in this life. Some will be given in the life to come. The Bible says, "No eye has seen, no ear has heard, no mind has conceived what God has prepared for those who love him."[9]

Serving Him out of duty or obligation becomes drudgery. Instead, our service should be the joy of our lives because of all He has done for us. As we serve Him, He sees every detail and knows just how He will reward us.

You and I have a reward waiting for us in Heaven. When we step through those gates of pearl . . . see the scars on His hands and His feet . . . see the love in His eyes . . . we will take the crowns He gives us in reward for our lives lived here for Him and lay them at His feet in worship! And regardless of how hard the work has been, at that moment it will be more than worth it. Because He is worth it!

Don't lose heart. Don't give up. Keep working hard for the Lord! He may reward you in some way on this earth, or He may reserve all of His reward to give you personally when you see Him face-to-face in Heaven. Remember, the real reward is Jesus. So stay motivated!

DAY 10 CHALLENGE

On this day, examine your motivation for service. Are you cheerfully serving as unto the Lord? Are you facing each day's difficulties in a way that honors Him, no matter how hard it is, knowing that this isn't all there is? If you are serving with anything less than a heart filled with love and gratitude for all He has done for you, ask Him to help you readjust. Don't miss out on the reward He wants to give you.

Lord of Glory,

You are the pearl of great price. You are Heaven's treasure. Forgive me for work done for You that has been perfunctory, mechanical, mindless, or heartless. Or done to impress others with how spiritual I am. As I take a good look at the cross and consider the work You did there for me, please accept my humble apology for the casual, negligent, or even prideful way I have done my work for You. I choose now to serve You not because I have to but because, with all my being, I want to repay the debt of love that I owe.

For the sake of the Bridegroom,
And in His name—Jesus,
Amen.

Unashamed

He asked, "Whose daughter are you? Please tell
me, is there room in your father's house for us to
spend the night?"

She answered him, "I am the daughter of
Bethuel, the son that Milcah bore to Nahor."

—Genesis 24:23–24

WHEN ABRAHAM'S SERVANT ASKED REBEKAH WHO
her father was, she didn't hesitate to tell him.
She didn't fumble with her words. She didn't turn
bright red and dismiss his question or change the sub-
ject. She didn't roll her eyes like he was crazy to assume she had a father. She didn't offer a vague response
like "He's just a man that lives nearby." She wasn't em-

barrassed to acknowledge his name. Instead, she answered with confidence and clarity.

You might think, *How silly. Of course she answered him. It wasn't a difficult question.* So why is it that we, as followers of Jesus, often hesitate to acknowledge our relationship with Him or speak His name when given the opportunity?

What is our response when someone asks us why we are so joyful today? Do we attribute our joy to the beautiful weather or the delicious tacos we just ate? Or do we declare that the real reason for our joy is that we have a heavenly Father who loves us? When someone at work makes a comment such as "How can anyone believe there is a God in this wicked world?" do we stay silent, maybe shake our heads and shrug? Or do we confidently and clearly give them the answer, saying something like "I believe it, and let me tell you why our wicked world needs Jesus."

Why do we ever hesitate to speak His name? Jesus said, "Whoever acknowledges me before men, I will also acknowledge him before my Father in heaven. But whoever disowns me before men, I will disown him before my Father in heaven."[1]

If you are afraid to speak Jesus's name in public or hesitant to let anyone know you are one of His followers, or if you've tried to talk about Jesus and failed for whatever reason, I want to encourage you through a principle my mom has shared with me.

When you and I fail to stand up and speak out, or fail in our attempt to do so, we need to acknowledge it to the Lord, then be on high alert, because very often He will give us another opportunity. It's almost, Mom says, as though failure is a setup for the opportunity that follows.

The apostle Peter, one of the twelve disciples of Jesus, learned this principle the hard way. On the night He was betrayed, Jesus told Peter that he would disown Him three times before the rooster crowed.[2] Peter adamantly insisted he would never do such a thing.[3] Of course, Jesus, who always speaks truth, was right. During the trials of Jesus, when Peter was confronted by a servant girl of the high priest, he denied Jesus, saying, "I don't know or understand what you're talking about." She again stated in front of people gathered around that he was a follower of Jesus, and he denied Jesus again. Then the people challenged him a third time, and he responded with curses and said, "I don't know this man you're talking about." The rooster crowed. And Peter, entering into a spiral of regret, wept bitterly and fled into the night.[4]

But when Jesus appeared to the disciples after the Resurrection, He talked with Peter. Instead of taking him out back and smacking him around, He lovingly asked three times if Peter loved Him, prompting the disciple to confess their relationship. And Peter was pulled up out of that spiral of depression. He was restored.[5] The opportunity that followed was history-making and history-changing, because God used Peter to establish His church.

If you've ever hesitated to declare your relationship with your heavenly Father or with His Son, Jesus, it's not the end of the story. Make it your priority that the next time you have an opportunity to speak His name, you'll do it—unashamedly! And why not? Think about it! He is the Creator and Sustainer of all things.[6] He is the Man who died for you. The One who has opened Heaven for you. He sits at God's right hand. All authority in the universe has been given to Him.[7] He is the Judge to whom one day everyone will give an account.[8] Hold your head up high! Speak His name with confidence!

Not long ago, I read an interview with a Nigerian man, Habila Adamu, who was unashamed to be identified with Jesus in the most terrifying situation. The terrorist group Boko Haram entered his house, demanding to know if he was a Christian or a Muslim. He answered that he was a follower of Jesus. They tried to get him to deny his faith in Jesus and convert to Islam. When he refused, they shot him point blank in the face and left him to die. He lay all night bleeding. His family thought he was dead, but he miraculously survived and has testified over and over about his love for Jesus and the miracle of his life.[9] He even said that he has forgiven his attackers and wishes to hug them, pray for them, and see them come to know Jesus![10]

You and I are unlikely to be confronted by a terrorist group like Habila was, but we encounter opportunities almost daily to speak up about Jesus. Most of the time it's in casual settings like at dinner with friends or while working alongside colleagues. During my second SCAD heart attack within a span of twenty-four hours, I was moments from dying and I knew it. Apparently seven nurses were in the room, stunned in bewilderment, not recognizing the symptoms of this very rare condition. I remember hearing my mom praying over me. As I began to slip away, I felt what I believe was the finger of God move across my heart. Immediately blood returned to my body and I was able to move and open my eyes. Before I could even think, the first thing that came out of my mouth with all the nurses standing around was "Jesus just saved my life! If you don't know Him, you need to!"

Jesus is our Healer, Protector, Defender, Creator, Sustainer, Comforter, Redeemer, Master, Rescuer, King of kings, and Lord of lords! How can we not shout His name from the rooftops? Be unashamed!

DAY 11 CHALLENGE

If the name of Jesus is not a regular part of your conversations, why not? Could it be that you need to cultivate an awareness of His presence that takes precedence over any situation or person you may confront? On this day, spend time in worship of Him; then tell one other person about Him and what He means to you. Just do it scared! It will become increasingly natural and habitual to talk of Him.

Lord Jesus,

I am so ashamed. Not of You, but of me and my reticence to speak publicly about You. I am so sorry. As I spend time every day listening for Your voice, as I read Your Word and talk to You in prayer, may my heart and mind be filled with thoughts of You. And then as I open my mouth, may those thoughts spill out in my conversations with genuine joy in who You are and gratitude for all You have done.

For the sake of the Bridegroom,
And in His name—Jesus,
Amen.

DAY 12

Hospitable

We have plenty of straw and fodder, as well as
room for you to spend the night.

—Genesis 24:25

ABRAHAM'S SERVANT AND THE MEN WHO HAD TRAVELED
with him needed a place to stay and didn't have
the convenience of calling ahead and reserving rooms
at a local inn. They had to rely on someone's hospitality, or they would end up sleeping on the city streets.
Rebekah graciously opened her family's home, and she
and her family used their resources to bless these trav-
elers.

Hospitality was ingrained in the culture of the ancient world, but for those who seek to please God today, it remains a high value. In his letter to the Romans, Paul urged, "Share with God's people who are in need. Practice hospitality."[1] And Peter, in one of his letters to the early church, anticipated our excuses with this instruction: "Offer hospitality to one another without grumbling."[2] Modern-day life can be so busy, busy, busy, that we need reminding to be welcoming to others.

My sister, Morrow, is the most hospitable person I have ever known! She and her husband, Traynor, have people over to their house for dinner several times a week. In addition, they host a couple of dozen young women each week for Bible study. The women are all excited to come into their home, because they know they are loved, welcomed, and sure to be well fed spiritually and physically.

Morrow uses the gift that God has given her to bless others, to open the door for sharing the gospel, and to simply love her guests because Jesus does. If you visit her house, you will feel like royalty. The second you walk in, she greets you with the kindest smile and somehow makes you feel like you can leave your worries at the door. Her house is peaceful and inviting. She always has something cooking on the stove or baking in the oven, filling the house with delicious aromas. If you come for dinner, one glance at her table is evidence that you have been thought about and planned for long before you arrived. There isn't a detail that she hasn't thought of. From the beautifully displayed dishes and floral arrangements, to the flickering candles, to the handwritten place card at each setting, you are assured that you've been expected and you are welcome. If you have the great privilege of spending the night, you will discover your bedcovers folded back with a chocolate on your pillow. The towels in the bathroom will be tied together with a pretty ribbon, and a small, wrapped gift will be placed at the end of the bed.

Morrow has told me before with delight in her eyes that every time she has someone in her home, she imagines she is serving Jesus. Which is exactly the attitude we are to have! Jesus said that when we receive others, it's as though we are receiving Him. And when we receive Him, we are really receiving His Father.[3]

Hospitality, regrettably, isn't something that comes easily to me. I absolutely love having people over to our home as much as possible, but I'm usually throwing things together at the last minute because I'm not a planner. Since noticing this about myself, I've begun to make more of an effort to thoughtfully prepare when I know company is coming.

The good news is that hospitality isn't about impressing people. It's a ministry! You and I may not have the time to have people over frequently, but when we do, we need to think like my sister, Morrow, being as hospitable as if Jesus were the honored guest, no matter how modest our home or our resources.

There is a wonderful story in the book of 2 Kings about a woman we know only as the Shunammite woman. She invited the prophet Elisha to dinner with her and her husband. She continued to host him for a meal each time he came through town. One day she told her husband that she wanted to add a little room with "a bed and a table, a chair and a lamp for him"[4] so that whenever Elisha came to town, he would have a place to stay that would essentially feel like home. Can you imagine the wonderful conversations the woman and her husband must have had with Elisha? They wanted to be a blessing to this amazing prophet of God, but I'm confident they were infinitely blessed themselves by having him in their home.

While I was growing up, my mom and dad had people in our home all the time. My mom is a marvelous southern cook, and everyone always devoured her food. But what I value most are the conversations that I sat and listened to, which were very instrumental in my walk with the Lord. So many times we had missionaries, friends from church, athletes from the local universities, ministry friends, and extended family sitting around our table and enjoying homemade pizza, homemade ice cream, homemade apple pie, or hamburgers from the grill. Sometimes her presentations were elegant, and sometimes they consisted of paper plates and cups, but the fellowship was always rich. It filled our home with life and laughter and love. I can't imagine all the conversations I would have missed, the relationships I wouldn't have had, if my mom hadn't been hospitable. I know it required putting forth effort in planning, shopping, cooking, and serving, but I'm so thankful that she did.

Sometimes you and I don't have the time to preplan, because, like with Abraham's servant, the need may arise suddenly, unexpectedly. Even if we have to wing it (which tends to be my style), we can still host others in a way that honors them and makes them feel special in our home. So why is this a big deal? A home that is welcoming and caring reflects the love of Jesus.

Who do you know that you could invite to your home for dinner? Someone who may be lonely and need Christian fellowship? Or do you know someone you can invite for a weekend stay who needs rest, just a break from their routine? Or is there a missionary family speaking at your church who needs rooms for several days while on furlough?

If you have teenage children, how can you make their friends feel welcomed and loved when they come to your house? For years I've been the chocolate-chip-cookie mom to many of my girls' friends. I love making cookies. It's something I know I can do. So the word is out that, every Friday night, whoever comes to our house will be treated to chocolate chip cookies as we embrace these young people for Jesus's sake.

Could you host a Bible study or prayer group in your home? In an intriguing, mysterious challenge to practice hospitality, we are encouraged by the writer of Hebrews to "keep on loving each other as brothers. Do not forget to entertain strangers, for by so doing some people have entertained angels without knowing it."[5] Wow! The implication is that Heaven is involved in our hospitality. We never know who we may bless or what blessing we may miss!

Can you imagine the blessing Rebekah would have missed had she and her family not opened their home to Abraham's servant? She would have missed untold wealth. She would have missed becoming Isaac's beloved wife. And she would have missed her son Jacob being in the lineage of the Messiah!

In these very last days, don't miss the blessing! Throw open the door of your heart and of your home. Be hospitable!

DAY 12 CHALLENGE

How are you using your home and resources to love others in the name of Jesus? Are you making excuses or making a difference? On this day, who can you invite to share a meal or cup of coffee? Ask God to bring a name to your mind, someone who would be blessed by your hospitality. Then pick up the phone and call or text them. Offer your home as a space where they feel safe, loved, and valued.

Lord of Heaven,

You gave Your very life to throw open Heaven's gates for me! Even now You are preparing a place for me so that when I walk through those gates, I will know I've come Home. I'm welcome. And I'm safe—forever. Thank You! Thank You!

Out of gratitude for Your divine hospitality, I want to show hospitality to others. Lead me to the people who need the encouragement and blessing of being at my table, in my kitchen, or on my porch. Then let Your love pour out through me to them so they are drawn irresistibly to You.

For the sake of the Bridegroom,
And in His name—Jesus,
Amen.

DAY 13

Eager to Share

The man bowed down and worshiped the LORD, saying, "Praise be to the LORD, the God of my master Abraham, who has not abandoned his kindness and faithfulness to my master. As for me, the LORD has led me on the journey to the house of my master's relatives."

The girl ran and told her mother's household about these things.

—Genesis 24:26–28

WHAT SHOCK AND AMAZEMENT REBEKAH MUST have felt when she heard the man pray and realized he was not a total stranger but the servant of her great-uncle Abraham! After watering ten thirsty camels, she would have been exhausted, so the fact that she ran to tell her family that Abraham's servant had come to see them shows how exciting this news was to her and how eager she was to share it.

There were no cellphones or any other kind of instant communication that Rebekah could have used to let her family know that company was on the way. I can't imagine it was a usual occurrence to have out-of-town relatives dropping in. Travel would have been difficult and dangerous. The rarity of this event would have made it all the more exciting!

Rebekah must have sprinted to the house, squealing with the news that a man from Abraham's household was just outside by the well. She must have breathlessly described the whole scene to her family while her new golden jewelry, given to her by Abraham's servant, glistened in the light of the cooking fire. Things would have immediately been put into motion while Rebekah's brother hurried out to greet their guest. The house must have been filled with the sound of pots clanging and knives chopping and serving pieces being placed on tables. The servants' chatter would have reverberated in the rooms as instructions were given, then hurriedly carried out. Many footsteps would have echoed down the corridors as servants rushed to prepare rooms and the banquet table. The excitement in the air would have been palpable!

In my mind's eye, what surely was an ordinary, colorless day in the life of this family was dramatically changed in an instant! God the Father, working through Abraham, his servant, and Rebekah herself, quickened the hearts of the entire family, preparing them to meet Abraham's servant . . . to listen to him . . . and, finally, to receive the message he had to share. When Rebekah ran to tell her mother, she had no way of knowing that the next few hours would change her life forever!

When was your heart quickened—stirred—by someone's testimony to the point you felt compelled to tell someone else of what you had heard? Did you feel drawn by the Father's Holy Servant to want to hear more? And invite others to hear more also? Was it a testimony at church? Or in a small group? Or in a neighborhood gathering? Was it a conversation with a pastor, a small-group leader, a parent, a friend, a coworker? Something you heard on the radio as you were driving? A time when someone shared such a specific answer to prayer that it was obvious only God could have intervened to answer?

In these last days, when the world is full of disheartening news, more than ever we need to join the psalmist in saying, "Come and listen, all you who fear God; let me tell you what he has done for me."[1] What a privilege we have to encourage others by sharing how God is at work in our lives and in the lives of others!

The apostle Paul himself, who encouraged others again and again, also needed encouragement. He wrote to the Roman followers of Jesus, whom he had never met, that their faith was being reported all over the world. Not only had that report motivated Paul to pray for the Romans, but he was also planning a visit so they could be mutually encouraged.[2] On another occasion, he commended the Corinthian church for their eagerness to help other followers of Jesus who were in need. He even stated that he was so blessed, he boasted about them.[3]

Recently my daughter Sophia called me from college. I could tell she was excited by the sound of her voice as she said, "Mom, you won't believe the conversation I just had!" She then proceeded to tell me about a study group where she planned to meet two other girls and study for a test. When she arrived, Sophia recognized that one of the girls was sharing with the other girl about God's love. Sophia's voice pulsated with emotion as she told me how academic studies were set aside as she joined the other believer in eagerly sharing with the third girl about God the Father's love for her. At the end of the three-hour conversation, the girl's heart began to open. Although she has yet to respond by receiving the Father's love, Sophia had the thrill of communicating in such a way that the girl's heart was stirred. And Sophia was encouraged.

Sophia's experience brings to mind Mary Magdalene. Following the crucifixion and burial of Jesus, Mary went to the tomb. After finding the stone removed from the entrance, she ran to tell the disciples that someone had stolen the body. She then returned to the tomb and looked inside. Her attention was directed to someone standing behind her, whom she thought to be the gardener. Then the "gardener" called her by her name. To say her heart was stirred would be an understatement. Mary's entire being must have reverberated as from an electrical shock! Because she recognized His voice—the voice of Jesus. He wasn't dead! He was alive, and He was near her, back in her life. He then commissioned her to go and tell His disciples what she'd seen and heard. While Mary surely didn't understand everything, she knew she'd had a divine encounter. So she ran and told the disciples. They thought she was just a hysterical woman and therefore didn't believe her.[4] But I'm quite sure it made no difference to Mary, because she had the unspeakable joy of telling others what she'd experienced.

Do you take joy in telling others how you are encountering God and what He is saying to you, whether through His Word, time in prayer, or other ways? Don't be hesitant! Be eager to run and tell others what you have heard or experienced. When Rebekah told her family about Abraham's servant, she relayed the story just as she'd experienced it. She must have told it with enthusiasm and excitement, because she "ran and told." She didn't hesitate or keep it to herself. She didn't put it off until it was more convenient, she was more rested, she had the time, or she understood more about it.

Be like Rebekah. You don't have to fully understand everything. Just go and share with someone "about these things"! And who knows? What you share may be exactly what they needed to hear for their own encouragement. Yours may not be the only life the Holy Servant wants to change. Be eager to share!

DAY 13 CHALLENGE

What has the Father's Holy Servant been saying to you or teaching you in recent days? Who has God placed in front of you who needs the encouragement of knowing that God is active in your life today? That He speaks through His Word? That He intervenes to answer prayer? How can you encourage your family, your friends, your study group, your colleagues, your doctors, your hairstylist or barber, by eagerly sharing what God has said or is doing in your life? On this day, just do it.

Father, Son, and Holy Spirit,

I worship You as the triune God who is one yet three in one. How I praise You for Your activity in my life. When I am weak, You give me strength. When I am down, You lift me up. When I am confused, You give me wisdom. When I am lost, You find me and give me direction. When I am lonely, You give me Your divine companionship. When I am afraid, You give me peace. When I am in despair, You give me hope.

Thank You for revealing Yourself and speaking to me through the pages of my Bible. Thank You for hearing and answering my prayers. I can't wait to tell others who You are and what You have done for me. I am eager to share.

For the sake of the Bridegroom,
And in His name—Jesus,
Amen.

DAY 14

Authentic

Rebekah had a brother named Laban, and he
hurried out to the man at the spring. As soon as he
had seen the nose ring, and the bracelets on his
sister's arms, and had heard Rebekah tell what the
man said to her, he went out to the man and
found him standing by the camels near the spring.
"Come, you who are blessed by the Lord," he
said. "Why are you standing out here? I have
prepared the house and a place for the camels."

—Genesis 24:29–31

YEARS AGO, MY GRANDMOTHER TAI TAI GAVE ME A
beautiful pink vase. I placed it on top of an old
farmhouse cabinet in which I stored china. It remained

there for years. Whenever I opened the cabinet doors, I did so very carefully. The vase tended to wobble. I didn't want it to fall, because it was so special to me.

Occasionally I used the vase for fresh flowers. One day I inspected it more closely and discovered a Chinese stamp on the bottom. I began to wonder if it might actually be a really nice vase, perhaps worth even more than its sentimental value to me. The raised cherry blossom designs that wove their way up the sides appeared to be hand painted. Sunlight shone through the porcelain, which I had learned is an important quality of fine china. I noticed how well preserved it seemed to be.

Suddenly I experienced a whole new appreciation for this object I had casually enjoyed simply because it was a pretty gift from my grandmother. I took some pictures of it and sent them off to an antiques appraiser. I anxiously awaited a response, wondering if the vase was from the Ming dynasty or at least a very old and valuable relic from the Far East. I was so afraid it might be damaged that I removed it from the top of the cabinet, careful not to jar it as I did so. Then I tucked it into a drawer where it would be safe. My girls began asking me with curiosity if I had heard from the appraiser. Finally, I did hear! To my utter astonishment—and, honestly, to some degree of disappointment—the appraiser said it was a reproduction that was worth about twenty-five dollars. We all cracked up!

My vase had the appearance of an authentic antique, but it was just an imitation of the real thing.

Like my vase, Rebekah's brother, Laban, was an imitation. He came across as charming, generous, and hospitable, but on closer inspection, he proved to be a phony.

The truth of his character became apparent years later when, in Genesis 29, Laban swindled Rebekah and Isaac's son Jacob. Laban promised to allow Jacob to marry his daughter Rachel in return for seven years of work. After the seven years were up, Laban tricked Jacob into marrying his daughter Leah. When Jacob confronted his new father-in-law, Laban said Jacob must work seven more years if he wanted to have Rachel as his wife. Laban heartlessly didn't care about either of his daughters or Jacob. He only wanted to increase his wealth through Jacob's service. He lied, manipulated, and even cheated all while putting on an air of sincerity.

Given that we know Laban was a greedy man, it seems obvious that it was Rebekah's jewelry, given to her by Abraham's servant, that drew her brother's interest. He took one look at the gifts from this stranger, and his eyes must have lit up with dollar signs! Or shekel signs. Recognizing an opportunity, he hurried out to the well to see the man, not necessarily out of authentic concern but because he was eager to see what he could gain from this visitor.

In contrast to Laban's offer of hospitality, Rebekah's service to the stranger was selfless and heartfelt. This brother and sister demonstrate the difference between an authentic Jesus follower and one who is faking it. And it's interesting to me that they were in the same family. With the same parents. Raised, I'm assuming, in the same way.

Imitation Christians may say the right things at church or in Bible study; they may act the right way in those settings; they may even pray in public, coming off as impressive and knowledgeable. But their faith is just a show. God rebuked such hypocrites in Isaiah 29:13: "These people come near to me with their mouth and honor me with their lips, but their hearts are far from me." Do you know people like that? People who put on a religious show but don't live out their faith from their hearts? People who lack a vibrant love relationship with God? Is it possible you are one? What is the true motivation driving your daily thoughts and behavior?

In Matthew 23:2–3, Jesus was very clear: "The teachers of the law and the Pharisees sit in Moses' seat. So you must obey them and do everything they tell you. But do not do what they do, for they do not practice what they preach." In other words, don't judge the truth of God's Word by the lie that people like the Pharisees are living. Jesus went on to verbally blister the Pharisees when He described them as white-washed tombs that were beautiful on the outside but filled with decay, explaining, "On the outside you appear to people as righteous but on the inside you are full of hypocrisy and wickedness."[1] Jesus was calling them out because they weren't authentic. They knew the law and taught the law, but it was all for show. There was no love in their hearts for the Lord.

People may call themselves Christians yet have no genuine holiness, righteousness, or love for the Lord in their hearts. Like Laban, they often serve for their own gain . . . to build their own reputation . . . to make social or business contacts . . . to appear to others as virtuous and spiritual . . . but God isn't first in their hearts. Consider the grief endured by individual followers of Jesus and the damage done to the credibility of the church because of the corrosive hypocrisy of clergy who commit sexual abuse, or pastors who have affairs with their secretaries, or ministries that amass large amounts of cash to spend on the luxurious lifestyle of their leaders. I seem to hear the words of Jesus reverberating: "Woe to you!"[2]

Closer to home, consider the effects when you and I allow the values of the world to lure us away from pure, heartfelt service to the Lord. In Romans 12, the apostle Paul urges us to be genuine in our love for the Lord and others, to "hate what is evil [and] cling to what is good."[3] He goes on to list the qualities that flow naturally from a heart conformed to God's will. A good measure of our true motivations is how well our lives align with Romans 12:9–21: "Love must be sincere. . . . Be devoted to one another in brotherly love. Honor one another above yourselves. Never be lacking in zeal, but keep your spiritual fervor, serving the Lord. Be joyful in hope, patient in affliction, faithful in prayer. Share with God's people who are in need. Practice hospitality. Bless those who persecute you; bless and do not curse. Rejoice with those who rejoice; mourn with those who mourn. Live in harmony with one another. Do not be proud, but be willing to associate with people of low position. Do not be conceited. Do not repay anyone evil for evil. Be careful to do what is right in the eyes of everybody. If it is possible, as far as it depends on you, live at peace with everyone. Do not take revenge, my friends, but leave room for God's wrath, for it is written: 'It is mine to avenge; I will repay,' says the Lord. On the contrary: 'If your enemy is hungry, feed him; if he is thirsty, give him something to drink. In doing this, you will heap burning coals on his head.' Do not be overcome by evil, but overcome evil with good."

That's almost an indictment of Christians today, isn't it? Who do you know who matches that description? One woman I know who does is Helen George, a modern-day Rebekah who has assisted my mom in ministry for more than forty-five years. It's been said that when my mom starts a sentence, Mrs. George can finish it! I was a newborn when she and my mom decided to step out in faith and start a Bible Study Fellowship class in our hometown. She served my mom in that class for twelve years as her administrative assistant; then when God called my mom into a full-time itinerant ministry, Mrs. George felt led to come alongside my mom and assist her.

From scheduling, to making phone calls, to writing letters, to answering emails and inquiries, to proofing many manuscripts before they are sent to the publisher, Mrs. George tirelessly serves. In all these years, I've never seen her without a smile. Literally—her resting face is a smile! Her joy is absolutely contagious. And her service is completely selfless. She jumps up to take care of everyone else, never thinking of herself. She has refused to receive a salary despite working full-time. She was my Sunday school teacher in elementary school and still teaches children in her church to this day. I've never seen anyone who serves more completely! And she always relies on Jesus. When her wonderful husband passed away, she told everyone in the months after his death how the Lord had become her husband—even to the point of helping her clasp a small necklace that was usually fastened by her husband. She wakes up early every morning to study the Word and spend time with God in prayer. She is a member of at least two weekly Bible studies. She speaks locally at various functions and is known as a prayer warrior. People regularly seek her wise counsel. Mrs. George is a genuine, clear reflection of Jesus.

Rather than being content to live as a cheap imitation like my vase or Laban, follow the example of Rebekah and Mrs. George. Be authentic.

DAY 14 CHALLENGE

Would those who know you best describe you in the same way that a casual acquaintance would? Think about the effort you expend to act or speak one way when you are with a particular group and another way when you are with a different group. It can be stressful and exhausting. It's so much easier to be real, to be the same in private as you are in public. So on this day, drop the mask and the pretense. Stop living to impress others, and instead, live to please God, 24/7.

Son of the Father,

I worship You as the authentic, exact representation of Your Father.[4] Your beloved disciple testified, "No one has ever seen God, but God the only Son, who is at the Father's side, has made him known."[5] Please cleanse me and fill me until others, including my own family and friends, look at me and see You.

For the sake of the Bridegroom,
And in His name—Jesus,
Amen.

A Good Listener

The man went to the house, and the camels were unloaded. Straw and fodder were brought for the camels, and water for him and his men to wash their feet. Then food was set before him, but he said, "I will not eat until I have told you what I have to say."

"Then tell us," Laban said.

—Genesis 24:32–33

ABRAHAM'S SERVANT AND THE MEN WHO TRAVELED with him were brought into the home of Rebekah's family. Their camels were given food, and the men were given water with which to bathe. Abraham's servant was invited to eat as the family gathered around. I wonder if they were unable to hide their curiosity, perhaps staring at the servant while the food filled the room with delicious aromas. Their stomachs must have been growling with hunger in anticipation of the food set before them.

Out of respect, the family waited for their honored guest to go first. It was then that Abraham's servant spoke. What he said must have given them pause. The man declined to eat. He set aside his own physical need for sustenance and refreshment after such a long journey, stating that before he took a bite, he wanted to relay his message. It soon became apparent to his listeners that he wasn't there by accident but that his long journey had a purpose that involved a dramatic and very specific answer to prayer.

I wonder if Rebekah was hovering around the dinner table, curious to discover what the stranger had to say. I expect she assumed what she was about to hear might be interesting but had nothing to do with her. Was she startled by the news that her great-uncle Abraham, now a very wealthy man, was seeking a bride for his son? From his own family—her family? Did her pulse quicken and her heart start to pound as the servant's eyes repeatedly returned to her and lingered on her face with fatherly affection? Finally, with a voice likely pulsating with emotion, the servant shared that she—*Rebekah!*—was God's miraculous answer to his prayer.

Surely she held her breath as she continued to listen. Was she stunned to learn that her service to him as she watered his camels was actually God supernaturally guiding her, indicating to the man that she was to be the bride for Isaac, Abraham's son? Did her entire world seem frozen in time as she realized that her life was about to radically change? That she would never be the same after this day?

If Rebekah and her family had chosen not to listen to the servant's story—if they had simply housed and fed him but not listened to what he had to say—think of the blessing they would have missed! Which makes me wonder, What blessing are we missing because we don't listen to the voice of God? Does the Lord want to tell us about our future, give answers to prayer, provide wisdom for decisions we are facing, reveal who He wants us to marry, and lead us to the job He has for us? What keeps us from listening? Are we too busy? Do we not know how to listen? Are we too prideful to hear? Too distracted? Too tired?

Recently I experienced severe heart pain because of my two previous SCAD heart attacks.

The pain was increasing to the point that I began to be fearful, wondering if another artery in my heart was about to dissect. I was watching the NCAA basketball national championship with my husband and youngest daughter, Riggin. I didn't want to worry them, so I prayed silently, asking God to relieve me of the pain. As I prayed, the Lord brought to my mind this verse: "Do not be anxious about anything, but in everything, by prayer and petition, with thanksgiving, present your requests to God. And the peace of God, which transcends all understanding, *will guard your hearts* and your minds in Christ Jesus."[1] I kept repeating that verse as I asked God to help me not be afraid.

The next morning in my devotions, the Lord led me to the verse in Isaiah that says, "Do not fear, for I am with you; do not be dismayed, for I am your God. I will strengthen you and help you; I will uphold you with my righteous right hand."[2] Again, God was encouraging me not to be afraid, assuring me that He would take care of me.

What happened next still amazes me! A dear family friend messaged me a video clip of my grandfather. As I watched the video, I couldn't believe my ears. Daddy Bill quoted those same two passages! He even said "will guard your hearts" twice in his authoritative preaching voice. It was as though God had leaned out of Heaven to confirm to me that those verses were His promises to me. I didn't need to fear. I would be okay! Listening to God speaking to me through His Word was the key that removed my anxious thoughts and fears, even when the pain lingered.

Think of all the people in Scripture who listened to

the voice of the Lord and the difference it made. Noah listened to the Lord, and the entire human race was saved during the worldwide flood.[3] Joseph listened as the Lord gave him the interpretation of Pharaoh's dreams, which resulted in his saving Egypt and his family during seven years of severe famine.[4] Moses listened to the voice of the Lord as He spoke through the burning bush, and God's people were delivered from slavery.[5] Joshua listened to the Lord and overcame the enemy stronghold of Jericho.[6] David listened to the Lord's instructions on how to defeat his enemies and became the greatest king of Israel.[7] The people in Nehemiah's day listened to God's Word as it was read aloud by Ezra, and they experienced national revival.[8] Saul of Tarsus listened to God speak to him on the Damascus Road and was radically transformed into the apostle Paul, a persecutor of Christians who became the greatest evangelist of all time.[9] The apostle John listened to God speak to him while in exile on Patmos and wrote down the end of God's story, which has given hope to every generation since.[10]

Again and again, Jesus told His followers who were gathered in seven different churches, "He who has an ear, let him hear what the Spirit says."[11] The five churches who didn't listen lie in ruins today. The two that did listen still have followers of Jesus two thousand years later.[12]

If Rebekah had chosen not to listen to what the servant was telling her, think of all she would have missed: a loving husband, untold wealth, a place in the genealogy of Jesus, and a name that is honored four thousand years later. If you and I choose not to listen to what God's Holy Servant says to us through His Word, think of all we will miss: wisdom for decisions, direction for life, effective guidelines for living, comfort in our grief, hope for the future, peace in our hearts, joy that is unrelated to our circumstances, and the list goes on.

In these last days when so many voices and deceiving spirits are trying to confuse, distract, and destroy us, you and I must make time to listen to the voice of God as He speaks through His Word. Just as Abraham's servant refused to eat until he had shared how God had answered his prayer, we also need to set aside anything that would distract us—eating, sleeping, talking, shopping, texting, emailing, television, appointments—in order to make time to listen to what God has to say as we read our Bibles. God wants to direct us, guide us, encourage us, correct us, comfort us, bless us, and, yes, even alert us to His imminent return.

What a thrill beyond thrills, that the God of the universe wants to speak to us! Be a good listener.

DAY 15 CHALLENGE

How do you read your Bible? Are you reading it just for facts and information? Are you reading it to check off a daily portion so you can get through it in one year? Instead, on this day, take a moment to pray before you read and ask God the Holy Spirit to speak to you through the pages. Then open your spiritual ears and listen.

Living Word,

While You used the wind, the earthquake, and the fire to get Elijah's attention, it was the gentle whisper of Your voice that spoke to him.[13] *And the prophet Ezekiel observed that it was when the mighty cherubim and seraphim lowered their wings and ceased all activity that You spoke out of Heaven.*[14] *So as I choose to be silent and still in Your presence, then open my Bible to read, let me hear the whisper of Your Spirit speaking to my heart.*

For the sake of the Bridegroom,
And in His name—Jesus,
Amen.

DAY 16

Submissive

"I bowed down and worshiped the Lord. I praised the Lord, the God of my master Abraham, who had led me on the right road to get the granddaughter of my master's brother for his son. Now if you will show kindness and faithfulness to my master, tell me; and if not, tell me, so I may know which way to turn."

Laban and Bethuel answered, "This is from the Lord; we can say nothing to you one way or the other. Here is Rebekah; take her and go, and let her become the wife of your master's son, as the Lord has directed."

—Genesis 24:48–51

*S*UBMISSION IS THE ONE WORD THAT CAUSES ALMOST every woman to cringe when we hear it. The women on both sides of our family are strong, assertive, and opinionated. We are not pansies or pushovers in the least. So when we hear someone talk about submission, warning bells echo in our brains, alerting us to a possible battle! I have also observed the men in my family struggling to relinquish their control, in whatever form, to someone else. Why?

I wonder if part of the reason is that we as sinful humans have gotten things messed up. Could it be that if husbands were to properly love their wives as Christ loved the church, if wives treated their husbands with respect, if bosses gave oversight to their employees with kindness, if fathers and mothers disciplined their children with unconditional love, patience, and forgiveness, then we would all gladly submit because we would trust the person we were submitting to?[1] Yet whether we do so gladly or not, in His great wisdom, God has established an order of authority. He calls us, as His children, to submit first to Him, then to the authorities that have been placed over us, and then to one another. Rebekah seems to exemplify the pattern God has established.

There is no record of Rebekah putting up a fight in this passage. When her brother and father answered Abraham's servant agreeably by basically saying, "Take her to Isaac," Rebekah didn't choke on her falafel, drop her fork, look daggers at them, and protest so loudly that the pyramids way down in Egypt crumbled! We would miss how truly remarkable her calm demeanor was if we just read this passage like a history text. But this was real life! One second, she was a young single girl who may have had a crush on some shepherd boy, and the next, she was betrothed to a total stranger in a foreign land. She didn't argue with her family, pepper the man with questions, or assert her rights. She just quietly submitted. Arranged marriages were the custom in that day, but was there more to it? Could it be that as she listened to the servant describe his journey and how God so clearly led him—answering every detail of the man's prayer—her heart began to quicken and warm to the path unfolding before her? Did she quietly submit without arguing or resisting, because she could clearly see that God Himself was at work? Was she beginning to open her heart and mind to the possibility that she was indeed the chosen bride to whom God had supernaturally led the servant? Whatever hopes filled her mind in that moment must have been accompanied by trepidation, yet she didn't let fear lead to defiance or resistance.

Rebekah's attitude reminds me of an incident years ago when my oldest daughter, Bell, was four years old. I received a call from her preschool teacher, who said that Bell had busted her chin open at recess and would need stitches. I jumped in my car at lightning speed and raced to the preschool. When I flung open the door of the school, she was waiting there for me, her big green eyes filled with tears as she held a tissue over her cut.

After we arrived at the clinic, the doctor walked into the exam room and very gruffly said that she would need stitches. Bell's eyes started to get teary as he laid her back on the table to begin the procedure. When he grabbed a needle to numb her chin, she began to wail. He did absolutely nothing to calm her fears! He was uncaring and extremely impatient, and this mama wasn't happy.

Without getting angry, I asked him to step outside for a minute and let me talk with her. When he left the room, I put my hands on either side of Bell's face and smiled at her. Tears were tumbling out of her eyes. I said, "Bell, do you remember when Joshua was about to cross the Jordan River with the Israelites and he was really terrified?"

"Yes," she said in a shaky voice.

"Do you remember how God told Joshua not to be afraid, not to be terrified, because He was with him?"[2]

Her lip was still trembling, but she said, "Yes."

"Bell," I said, "God is telling you right now, you don't have to be afraid or terrified! He is with you and will protect you even though it's scary!"

She looked at me with her big, beautiful, teary eyes and said, "Okay, Mommy."

The doctor came back into the room to complete the procedure, and I saw Bell brace herself like a soldier. Her lip kept trembling, tears rolled down her face, but she didn't make a peep. The pediatrician gave her fifteen shots in the chin. Fifteen! But Bell took it like a champ. He sewed her up, and to this day, she has a little scar as a reminder of her courage to submit to a frightening procedure.

The doctor wasn't a person anyone would want to submit to, but when Bell realized that she could ultimately submit to and trust God in this situation, she was able to handle it. And that truth is one you and I can grab hold of when it's time to surrender to Him.

Life can be difficult. People can be difficult. Circumstances can be difficult. But no matter what comes our way, no matter how we are treated, when we remember that we submit to a loving, caring, protective heavenly Father, we can trust Him to know what is best. He will see us through all of life. So while He may allow bad things to happen to us, He will guide us through them—and out of them if they aren't for our ultimate good.[3]

Jesus Himself set a powerful example of submission. When in the Garden of Gethsemane, facing arrest, trials, then torture that culminated in His crucifixion, He prayed, "My Father, if it is possible, may this cup be taken from me. Yet not as I will, but as you will."[4] He submitted to His Father's will. I can't begin to imagine what would have happened if Jesus had refused to submit to His Father's will, excusing Himself from surrender because the plan was being carried out by jealous religious leaders, prideful politicians, an angry mob, and cruel soldiers. Instead, His death atoned for our sin. By His blood we are redeemed and justified before a holy God.[5]

Can you truly say you trust God enough to submit, whatever He asks of you? What has God been saying to you through His Word? Has He been speaking to you through the story of Rebekah about some area of your life that hasn't been submitted to Him? Are you in a relationship that isn't pleasing to the Lord? Are you not waiting on your Isaac or your Rebekah? Did your spouse get a job transfer out of state and you are resisting having to move? Whatever it is, have you been fighting Him on it? Wrestling with what you know is His will yet not what you want? Will you choose to submit to your loving heavenly Father and trust His plan for your life?

Rebekah became convinced that it was God's will for her to marry Isaac, which gave her peace as she trusted Him. So, too, when God calls us to walk an uncertain or difficult path, we can rest in the promise of His help and presence.[6] When we have a mean doctor or a difficult spouse or an unreasonable boss, we can seek God's guidance through Scripture, rest in His promises, and submit to His will and His plan for our lives.

As the return of the Bridegroom approaches, I pray He find us, like Rebekah, surrendered to Him so that on that day we will have no regrets! He knows best. So be submissive.

DAY 16 CHALLENGE

Who is in authority over you? What is your attitude toward that person? What difference would it make in your relationship if you were respectful . . . kind . . . considerate . . . submissive? And what difference would it make in your relationship with God if, instead of resisting, resenting, or even rebelling against His will, you submitted to it? On this day, ask God to give you an undivided heart of devoted trust in Him and put a new spirit within you.[7] Ask Him to remove any hardness and give you a soft heart.[8]

Master. Teacher.

*I worship You as One who lived in the glory of
Heaven, surrounded by adoring angels, yet came
to earth and got dirt on Your hands. Even as You
washed the grimy feet of Your disciples, You commanded them to follow Your example and do what
You have done.[9] So I choose to submit to You. I
submit my thoughts, my words, my actions, my
emotions, and my will to You. Because I trust the
One who submitted Himself for me.*

*For the sake of the Bridegroom,
And in His name—Jesus,
Amen.*

~~~~~~~

A Blessing to Others

The servant brought out gold and silver jewelry and articles of clothing and gave them to Rebekah; he also gave costly gifts to her brother and to her mother.

—Genesis 24:53

WITH THE SERVANT ON PRAYERFUL ALERT FOR THE perfect bride for his master's son, Rebekah's selfless service got his attention. If she had been rude, self-centered, or lazy, she surely would have been overlooked. But when her suitability was confirmed by her humility, sacrificial service, and family ties, she was chosen to be the bride. The servant showered her with a small fortune in extravagant jewelry and fine clothing. And then, for her sake, he gave an abundance of valuable gifts to her family.

One of the joys we have through being the chosen bride of the Father's Son is that we become a blessing to those around us. Our families reap the benefit when we are patient in stressful situations, when we are joyful even after a long, hard day, when we show love to a difficult child, when we cook or clean without complaining, when we are tender and compassionate toward a family member who is cranky when suffering, when we forgive a spouse who has said something hurtful—and the list goes on. All these beautiful behaviors are like jewels of blessing to our families!

At the house where I grew up, a water pump was attached to the well. To get water directly from the well, we would work the handle until the water flowed out. It required effort and good old elbow grease. Living for Jesus also requires effort. But the reward comes when the blessings flow to those around us.

The story is told of a little girl who questioned her pastor when she was confused by his sermon. He'd said she could ask Jesus to come live inside her heart. But then she inquired, "Isn't Jesus a man living up in Heaven?" When the pastor replied that He is, the little girl exclaimed that if she invited Him to live inside her, He would be sticking out all over! And the pastor responded emphatically, "That's right!" The same thing is true for you and me: If we have invited Jesus to live inside us, people should see Him "sticking out all over" by the way we handle situations and interactions all throughout the day.

The apostle Peter, who tended to be an impulsive hothead when he was younger, wrote these instructions toward the end of his life to followers of Jesus: "All of you, live in harmony with one another; be sympathetic, love as brothers, be compassionate and humble. Do not repay evil with evil or insult with insult, but with blessing, because to this you were called so that you may inherit a blessing."[1]

Interestingly, two bodies of water in Israel serve as a visual reminder of the challenge Peter gave to be a blessing as well as receive a blessing. Both seas receive water from the Jordan River. But while the river flows in and through the Sea of Galilee, it ends at the Dead Sea, where it becomes stagnant because there is no outlet. Likewise, if all we ever do is receive God's blessings without passing them on to others, we, too, will become spiritually stagnant . . . unfruitful . . . dead.

We find a beautiful, poignant example in the Old Testament of someone who was not stagnant but served as a blessing. David and his men were camped near a wealthy man named Nabal. They had watched over Nabal's shepherds and sheep, protecting them from enemy attack. One day David sent some of his men to ask Nabal to give them food in return for the kindness they had shown. The Bible describes Nabal as "surly and mean in his dealings."[2] True to his character, or lack of it, Nabal rudely said no in a way that was very disrespectful to David. When the men reported to David, he became so angry that he gathered four hundred of his men to attack Nabal and his household, determined to wipe out every man.

But that was when Abigail stepped into the story. She was the beautiful, kind, and wise woman who was married to the wretched Nabal. One of her servants reported how arrogantly her husband had refused David's men. The servant also described how good David and his men had been to them. Then he warned her that disaster was coming on the entire household as a result of her wicked husband.

Abigail quickly went to work. She gathered mountains of food, loaded it all up on donkeys, and traveled with her servants to meet David. How terrifying and intimidating it would have been to see the mighty David and his powerful army of men coming straight at her! But Abigail didn't hesitate or shrink back. She got off her donkey and bowed down at David's feet. She poured out her heart, selflessly saying she would take the blame and begging him not to sully his own name or hinder the Lord's blessing in his life by needless killings. She offered David the abundance of food she'd brought and pleaded with him to forgive her husband and her household for their offense toward him.

With such a wicked husband, Abigail had every reason to be bitter and miserable. She could have taken her favorite servants, hidden in a ravine, and allowed her husband to be killed, thus being set free from his abuse. Instead, she acted in a godly way. As she interceded for her husband, David was so moved by her humility, kindness, and sweet sincerity that he accepted her abundant gifts of food and told her to "go home in peace."[3] As a result, her husband and her household were saved from slaughter. And David was saved from taking vengeance that surely would have deeply wounded his conscience . . . and his reputation. Abigail was a blessing to her wicked husband and to the man who would become the greatest king of Israel. The beauty of the story is that not only was Abigail a blessing but she was also blessed in turn. When she told Nabal the next day what had transpired, he apparently had a stroke, and ten days later he died. When David heard about it, he sent for Abigail, asking her to be his wife, and she agreed.

Even if those in your home, extended family, school, neighborhood, or church are somewhat like Nabal, God has treasures of blessings He wants to pour out on you and then to them through you! Jesus Himself presented a radically unconventional way to handle the Nabals in our lives: "Love your enemies and pray for those who persecute you, that you may be sons of your Father in heaven."[4] And He assures us, "Blessed are you when people insult you, persecute you and falsely say all kinds of evil against you because of me. Rejoice and be glad, because great is your reward in heaven."[5]

I want to be a "son" of my Father in Heaven. Don't you? I want to be like Rebekah, who was a blessing to those around her. So let's make the commitment to be so filled up with Jesus and His Word—receiving His gifts of love, joy, peace, patience, kindness, goodness, faithfulness, gentleness, and self-control—that we overflow.[6] Don't become spiritually stagnant. Choose to receive the Father's blessings; then share with others what He has given you.

You've been blessed. Now be a blessing.

DAY 17 CHALLENGE

Is Jesus sticking out all over you? How would your family, friends, and co-workers answer that question? Examine your daily interactions. How has God blessed you, and how are you sharing those blessings with others? On this day, ask God to open your eyes to fresh opportunities to bless people in the name of Jesus. Then do so.

Enthroned Lord,

You are the Fountainhead of all blessing. The river of life-giving blessing flows from Your throne. One day that river will bring healing to the nations.[7] Yet even now, as I enthrone You in my heart, I pray that Your blessings will flow in me and through me to a spiritually drought-stricken world. Thank You for Your blessings. I'm sorry for the times I've hoarded them. Give me eyes to see those around me who desperately need Your blessings. Then stir my heart to share what You've given me and what You will also give them.

For the sake of the Bridegroom,
And in His name—Jesus,
Amen.

DAY 18

Committed

He said to them, "Do not detain me, now that the
Lord has granted success to my journey. Send me
on my way so I may go to my master."

Then they said, "Let's call the girl and ask her
about it." So they called Rebekah and asked her,
"Will you go with this man?"

"I will go," she said.

—Genesis 24:56–58

WE FACE MULTIPLE CHOICES EVERY DAY. WE CHOOSE
what to wear, what to eat, who to talk to, how
hard to work, and the list goes on. But in light of
eternity—thinking about Jesus getting ready to come
for His bride—we need to take a laser-focused look at

the choices we are making on a daily basis. Bottom line: Are they right choices? Do they match up with God's Word and His will? And once we have made each choice, how committed are we to following through with it?

One day Rebekah was a teenage girl doing chores in her family home; the next day she faced the life-shaping choice to either stay with her family or go to a foreign land to become the bride of the father's son. Her answer was simple, clear, and definite. There was no hesitation, ambiguity, or procrastination. She made the very difficult choice to leave her family and friends and go with the father's servant to marry a man she had never met. After hearing the servant tell the whole story of Abraham's instructions, his journey, and then his encounter with her at the well, she must have come to the realization that she had indeed been chosen to be Isaac's bride. But she also had to choose. Faced with such a monumental, life-altering decision, Rebekah made the right choice. She chose God's will and plan for her life, no matter what her own plans or dreams may have been up to that point. And she committed to following through with it.

We see all through Scripture that wrong choices can bring about negative consequences. Adam and Eve chose to disobey God and eat the forbidden fruit in the garden. They were banished from the garden

and brought sin and death into the world.[1] Cain chose
to not offer the blood sacrifice God required. He then
became jealous of his brother, Abel, and murdered
him. Cain was cursed for the rest of his life.[2] Abraham
and Sarah chose to have a son through a slave woman
instead of waiting on God, and the consequences have
included wars and hostility between the two sons and
their descendants until this day.[3] Ananias and Sap-
phira chose to lie about the money they gave to the
apostles, and they both died suddenly.[4]

While wrong choices can bring about destruction
in our lives and the lives of those around us, Scripture
also shows us the blessing and peace that come when
we make right choices and follow through with them.
Moses chose to obey God by confronting Pharaoh over
and over until the Israelites were set free.[5] Then he
committed himself to following through by leading
them out of Egypt, through the Red Sea, and to the
Promised Land. David chose to fight Goliath rather
than watch him defy the armies of God, saving the Israelites from the Philistines.[6] Shadrach, Meshach, and
Abednego refused to bow down in worship of King
Nebuchadnezzar's golden statue, then followed
through in commitment even though they were thrown
into the fiery furnace. The result was that they were
dramatically saved and the king worshipped God.[7]
Daniel chose to pray to God, keeping his commitment

to pray three times a day, even though he knew he would be thrown into a pit of lions. God shut the lions' mouths and delivered Daniel. As a result, King Darius glorified Daniel's God.[8] Paul and Silas chose to praise God, then stay in prison even when an earthquake loosened their chains. Their commitment led to the salvation of the jailer and his family.[9]

What choices have you made that have altered your life for good or for bad? The narrative in our world today is to follow your heart, to choose whatever makes you happy, feels good, or works to your advantage. Even if it's drugs, alcohol, an affair, a golf game over family time, spending more money than you have, or quitting school or a job—anything in the pursuit of happiness, pleasure, or personal advancement. Jesus tells us, "If anyone would come after me, he must deny himself and take up his cross and follow me. For whoever wants to save his life will lose it, but whoever loses his life for me will find it."[10]

Every day we have choices. Will they match up with His will, and how committed are we to really following through?

We have all made New Year's resolutions. We resolve to go on a diet, to stop drinking soda, to cut out desserts, to exercise more. But by February, how many of us have truly followed through?

After listening to the stranger, Rebekah knew that

God was leading her to marry Isaac, so she had peace knowing she was in God's will. She made the choice to go with Abraham's servant. But that choice was followed by a commitment to climb up on the back of a camel and ride for approximately 450 miles!

While life is filled with a multitude of decisions every day, there is one that is preeminent. You have been chosen by God the Father to be a bride that is pleasing to Him and to His Son, but it's also your choice. If you choose to be a bride worthy of the Bridegroom, it will be a life-changing decision. You will have to forsake your own plans and dreams, surrender your own will and goals, and "go with this man" every day for the rest of your life until you actually arrive with the Holy Servant at the Home that has been prepared for you. So the question is, "Will you go with this man?"

Since we are now on day 18 of this twenty-one-day challenge, I'm assuming you have made that choice. But how committed are you to following through in developing each of the previous seventeen characteristics of the bride the Father is seeking?

DAY 18 CHALLENGE

Go back over each of the previous seventeen characteristics of the bride the Father is seeking for His Son. Are you assured you are a family member? How faithful are you in the day-to-day? Are you beautiful on the inside? Purified? Spiritually filled? Kind? Do you have a servant's heart? How responsive are you to the needs of others? Are you honest? Motivated? Unashamed? Hospitable? Eager to share? Authentic? A good listener? Submissive? A blessing to others? Take inventory of the characteristics you need to develop more fully as well as the ones you lack. On this day, as you prepare to meet Jesus, make the commitment to work on each one so that you are pleasing to the Bridegroom.

Father of the Bridegroom,

     I stand amazed that You have chosen me. If I had another lifetime to live, it wouldn't be enough time to become all I should be in order to be worthy of Your choice. I am humbled and deeply grateful. So now I choose every day to follow through with heartfelt commitment to "go with this man" until Jesus comes for me in my death or at His return. I claim Your promise that as I am intentional in this commitment, You will transform me into His image with ever-increasing glory through the indwelling work of Your Spirit.[11] And I believe that You are able to keep that which I have committed until that Day.[12]

     For the sake of the Bridegroom,
     And in His name—Jesus,
     Amen.

DAY 19

Perseverant

Rebekah and her maids got ready and mounted
their camels and went back with the man. So the
servant took Rebekah and left.

—Genesis 24:61

REBEKAH'S CHOICE TO GO WITH THE SERVANT AND
become Isaac's bride required that she take a journey of approximately 450 miles—on a camel!—with
Abraham's servant to manage, lead, and care for her.

What must the journey have been like? It began on
the morning Rebekah agreed to go.[1] The sun would
have just been peeking up over the desert horizon,
promising a cloudless, hot day. The camels were pa-

tiently waiting to begin the journey with heavy packs hanging on their sides, filled to the brim with Rebekah's belongings. This wasn't a "see you in a couple of months" kind of trip. Rebekah probably would never see her loved ones again. As her family spoke words of blessing, I wonder if she was fighting back tears. But she courageously said her goodbyes and climbed onto the back of a camel. Her nurse may have been already perched on her camel, possibly feeling excited but feeling anxious also, as she, too, was leaving all that was familiar.[2] Then with a command from one of the men, the camels rose awkwardly to their feet. Rebekah's camel would have lurched forward, then backward as it finally stood on all fours. As the caravan moved out, Rebekah would have swayed with the steady rhythm of the camel's unique stride. Her journey to a new life had begun.

When you and I agree to "go with this man," committing ourselves to being the bride of the Father's Son, we, too, begin a journey that continues for a lifetime. While the journey is different for each of us, it includes good times and bad, challenges and crises, hardships and pain, as well as the joyous expectation of the end when we meet our Bridegroom face-to-face. It calls for perseverance in order to arrive at our destination. But make no mistake: The Holy Servant never leaves our side.

My journey has included many difficulties and has required daily perseverance. While I was in high school, the Lord gave me 1 Peter 4:12–13 as my life verses: "Dear friends, do not be surprised at the painful trial you are suffering, as though something strange were happening to you. But rejoice that you participate in the sufferings of Christ, so that you may be overjoyed when his glory is revealed." I had no idea as a teenager the many painful trials that I would face in life. Yet they pale in comparison with the intensity and frequency of the trials that I have encountered this past year. It may be that whatever I'm going through in the present seems worse than the difficulties in the past. But through this entire journey, *God has been with me!*

The Holy Spirit has comforted me when I've been in tears. He literally saved me when I was dying. He's spoken to me multiple times through Scripture, giving me promises to claim that have filled me with peace when things looked hopeless. He's given me extreme strength and self-control when my flesh wanted to lash out. He's given me wisdom when I've had to counsel hard hearts and broken hearts. He's reminded me of the suffering Jesus went through, assuring me that He understands. He's encouraged me so much, reminding me that He is the God who sees me.[3] He's blessed me on the difficult days with unexpected snow showers or a cozy rainy afternoon or warm sun on my face. He's lifted my spirits by bringing to mind the lyrics of praise songs. He's calmed my fears through His Word when my physical heart pain has seemed endless. I know I'm on a lifelong journey with the Holy Servant leading me, teaching me, guiding me, counseling me, comforting me, and strengthening me through whatever the difficulty may be as I draw closer and closer to my Bridegroom . . . Jesus. With all my heart, I want to be prepared to be His bride!

As Rebekah persevered on her journey, I wonder when she began to question the servant. Once they were well on their way and the tears stopped flowing, did Rebekah's anticipation of her future cause thoughts of her past, and all she had left behind, to fade? With curiosity she must have sidled her camel up to the old servant and summoned the courage to ask the kind man about Isaac. "What does he look like? What does his voice sound like? Is he quiet or talkative? Does he have a good relationship with his parents? Is he protective? Is he kind? What does he like to do? What does the land look like where we are going? What is my uncle Abraham like? Will they be pleased with me?"

I picture the faithful old servant with wrinkles that creased the corners of his eyes when he smiled. I'm sure he encouraged Rebekah's perseverance by filling her in on the details of how God called Abraham to leave his country, his people, and his father's house and how he followed God in obedience, just as she was doing.[4] And surely he told Rebekah about Isaac's miraculous conception and birth, that he was the fulfillment of God's promise to Sarah and Abraham. I wonder if he shared with her about Abraham's obedience to God above all else even to the point of being willing to sacrifice his beloved only son. And he must have told her about Isaac's beautiful submission to his father.[5] Did he also tell her about Isaac's half brother, Ishmael, and what their relationship was like?

As Rebekah listened to the servant, did she begin to fall in love with Isaac before she even laid eyes on him? With all the time they had on their journey, I'm sure the servant went into great detail, so much so that Rebekah must have felt as if she already knew Isaac, could already picture him in her head, could already imagine looking into his loving face, could already feel the excitement and honor of being his bride.

On our journey we have the opportunity to open our Bibles and listen to the Holy Servant as He begins revealing to us who our Bridegroom is. The apostle John lovingly encourages followers of Jesus, calling us "dear children," then exhorting us to "continue in him, so that when he appears we may be confident and unashamed before him at his coming."[6] Our hearts should quicken at the sound of His great name as we hear about how He healed the lame, loved the little children, defended the weak, spoke wisely in the face of anger, cast out demons, withstood temptation in the desert, fed the five thousand, raised the dead, lived a sinless life, loved us so much that He died a gruesome death on a Roman cross to take God's judgment in our place, was raised to life on the third day to offer us eternal life and open Heaven for us, and is now seated at the right hand of God the Father, preparing to return and take us to live with Him forever. As we eagerly seek to learn all this and more about Jesus, then our hearts, like Rebekah's, will fall deeper and deeper in love with our Bridegroom, even before we've laid eyes on Him!

As Rebekah's camel drew nearer to her destination, her expectancy must have been heightened to the point she couldn't take her eyes off the horizon. She was so close to meeting Isaac face-to-face.

I believe the end of our journey may be nearer than we think. I can hardly take my eyes off the horizon as I match biblical prophecies with events taking place in our world today. This is one reason my mother and I are writing this book: We want to be prepared to meet Jesus, and we want *you* to be prepared to meet Him also, whenever He comes. For each of us, this calls for a lifetime of perseverance!

DAY 19 CHALLENGE

If you are not falling more and more in love with the Bride-groom, if you are not filled with the anticipation of seeing Him face-to-face, then I wonder . . . Like the Ephesians, have you put your work, activity, and busyness before your worship?[7] Before starting this twenty-one-day journey, have you been inconsistent in your Bible reading, prayer, obedience, and fellowship with other Jesus followers? Use the challenge of this journey to be like a new bride. Seek to learn more about Jesus, meeting Him in prayer and through the pages of your Bible. Ask the Holy Servant to reveal to you His character, His likes and dislikes, His plans and purposes, and, above all, His love for you. Don't waste the journey. Persevere as you make every step count.

Eternal Lord,

I worship You for Your persevering commitment to me that began before the worlds were created, that carried You from Heaven's throne to earth's cradle, that led You to stay on the cross until You gave Your life for me, then rise up from the dead to sit at the Father's right hand, where even now You pray for me without ceasing[8]—a faithful perseverance that one day will climax when You return to take me to the Home You have prepared. For me!

Please don't let me waste my life's journey. As I choose to persevere, make me more mindful of the Holy Servant, who is not just at my side but who indwells me. Give me strength, stamina, courage, and faithfulness for each step of the journey. Until I see You face-to-face.

For the sake of the Bridegroom,
And in His name—Jesus,
Amen.

DAY 20

Focused

[Isaac] went out to the field one evening to
meditate, and as he looked up, he saw camels
approaching. Rebekah also looked up and saw
Isaac. She got down from her camel and asked the
servant, "Who is that man in the field coming to
meet us?"

"He is my master," the servant answered.

—Genesis 24:63–65

AS THE SERVANT AND REBEKAH JOURNEYED CLOSER
and closer to their destination, he must have
pointed out landmarks to let her know they were drawing near. Think of the significance of all those places:
the great tree in Shechem where the Lord appeared to

Abraham when he first entered Canaan;[1] the place where Abraham entered into a covenant with the Lord and learned that he and his wife, Sarah, would have a son the following year at the ages of one hundred and ninety, respectively;[2] Bethel, where Abraham returned after his dramatic failure in Egypt;[3] Mount Moriah, the place of Abraham's sacrifice of Isaac;[4] the cave of Machpelah, where Abraham's beautiful wife and Isaac's beloved mother was buried;[5] and he may have even told her about the charred fields that once had been Sodom and Gomorrah.[6]

As Rebekah listened to the rhythm of the camels' hooves padding across the terrain, felt the warmth of the sun beating down on her back, and took in the sights of the new land she was entering, never could she have fathomed the significance of her place in human history. Can you imagine the army of angels assigned to guard her on the journey? Or the electric excitement in the heavenly realms as God's redemptive story continued to unfold through the first meeting of Abraham's promised son, Isaac, and his new bride, Rebekah—a union that would ultimately lead to the birth of Jesus? It's almost as if creation itself held its breath as the moment drew near!

The twilight of the evening would have cast a soft glow over the land as Isaac went out in the field to pray. I wonder if he was praying for his future bride, anticipating the moment of their first meeting. Was he asking God to protect her, to prepare her heart to meet him, to help her fall in love with him before they laid eyes on each other, to cause her to long for him as he longed for her? Had he gone out to the field each day and watched for her in the distance, straining his eyes, feeling his heart quicken at the thought of her arrival? And on this particular night, at what point in his prayer did he look up? His breath must have caught when he saw her, and his heart must have raced at the realization that she had arrived! I imagine, with his broad shoulders and confident stride, he quickly went to meet her, so overwhelmed that at last God had indeed provided a bride!

In those same moments Rebekah could have been so weary from the journey that she slumped on the camel's back. Her eyes could have been downcast because of exhaustion and the strain of looking for Isaac day after day, week after week. Instead, Rebekah apparently was still intently focused as she kept looking for her bridegroom. As evening settled over the desert landscape, I wonder if she was aware of how sore her shoulders were, how strained her eyes felt. Yet she kept looking expectantly toward the horizon. Maybe she rubbed her eyes, squinting to focus more clearly. And then—was it a nudge from the Holy Spirit, a stirring in her heart, an awakening in her soul, a thrilling shiver through her tired body? Someone was indeed coming straight toward her!

The servant must have almost burst with excitement as he waited for Rebekah to comment on Isaac's presence in the distance. When she asked who the man was, he replied simply, "He is my master."[7] Then she knew—the man she had grown to love and longed to meet face-to-face was right there! No more waiting, no more longing, no more imagining. No more agonizing, weary journey. He was right there before her eyes. In the flesh! She quickly covered herself with her veil. I wonder why. Was she suddenly shy, afraid she wouldn't be pleasing to Isaac? Was she being modest? Was she letting him know that she was the bride? Maybe it was to cover an unbridled love that beamed from her eyes and caused her lips to part in breathless wonder. Whatever the reason, there must have been ecstatic joy, heavenly fireworks, soaring elation, as the faithful servant presented the chosen bride to the father's son.

There is a story told years ago of a blind man who graduated from college with honors despite his impairment. But more important, he had won the heart of a beautiful young lady to whom he was engaged to be married. Before the big wedding day, he underwent several procedures to try to regain his sight, which he'd lost at the age of ten because of an unfortunate accident. I can imagine the excitement and trepidation tangled up in his hope that the procedures would bring about success. The couple decided that the big reveal would be on their wedding day.

When that day finally arrived, his father drove him to the church, which was filled with all sorts of dignitaries, leaders, and friends. With bandages still covering his eyes, they led him into the sanctuary. The wedding march began, and the bride made her way down the aisle. Surely her heart must have been beating out of her chest as she wondered if her beloved would be able to see her face with his eyes and not just his hands. When she neared the front of the church, she saw her groom standing with his father and his doctor. There must have been a hush in the room as everyone, including the bride, held their breath and watched the doctor cut away the bandages. And then the moment came when the last bandage fell off!

The groom's eyes found hers, and with absolute elation he walked to her, drinking in the beauty of her face. It was told that when he reached her, the bride said, "At last!" and the groom echoed, "At last."[8]

Oh, dear believer, the significance of this story is beyond imagination! Jesus, your Bridegroom, is in His heavenly Home awaiting you, His bride! Just as Isaac was praying in the fields by his home, Jesus is praying for you.[9] Praying that you would long for Him. Praying for protection on your journey.[10] Praying that your heart would be prepared to see Him. Praying that you would fall deeper and deeper in love with Him even though you haven't seen Him face-to-face.[11]

He tells us in Scripture that "no one knows about that day or hour, not even the angels in heaven, nor the Son, but only the Father."[12] He is watching and waiting for the moment when God the Father says, "It's time!" Then, in a flash, in the twinkling of an eye, Paul tells us, "the Lord *himself* will come down from heaven, with a loud command, with the voice of the archangel and with the trumpet call of God, and the dead in Christ will rise first. After that, we who are still alive and are left will be caught up with them in the clouds to meet the Lord in the air. And so we will be with the Lord forever. Therefore encourage each other with these words."[13]

He is coming! The time is drawing near. The excitement in Heaven must be electric in anticipation of the wedding that is soon to take place. Soon you will see the joy on your Bridegroom's face and the love in His eyes for you . . . His bride!

Like Abraham's servant accompanying Rebekah, the dear Holy Servant has been guiding us on our journey. He's given us signs to let us know that the time is drawing near. Jesus Himself told us over and over that we need to be watchful! Don't let it catch you off guard like a thief in the night.[14]

Our journey might be difficult, and the road might be long, as Rebekah's was, but we are never to lose sight of what is at the end of our journey. "Let us fix our eyes on Jesus, the author and perfecter of our faith."[15] Our focus needs to be on Him, not on all the distractions and temptations, the weariness and busyness, the fears and failures, the discouragements and disappointments, we face in the world. Don't slump down in weariness and take your eyes off the horizon. As believers, we are commanded to watch as we anticipate the moment when our eyes finally see Jesus.[16] So . . . stay focused!

DAY 20 CHALLENGE

On what are you focused? Is it your trials and disappointments? The deferred dream? The goal that seems just within reach? The wickedness of the world or the complacency in the church? On this next-to-the-last day of our challenge, refocus on the horizon, looking expectantly, eagerly, for the return of Jesus. Take time today to read the signs He gave in Matthew 24 that indicate His return is near. Don't be distracted by the glittery temptations of this world, and don't allow yourself to slump into apathy or discouragement. Instead, keep looking up. The Bridegroom is coming—for you!

Living Lord, Returning King,

    I have looked for You until I feel my spiritual eyes are strained. I have read the signs You have given that indicate Your return, and they match what I see taking place in the world around me. I have a growing expectancy that at any moment I'm going to see You face-to-face. My heart is yearning for You! I long to see the expression on Your face when You see those I have led to put their trust in You. Especially those in my family. I long to feel Your touch, to hear Your audible voice. Please use the intensity of my expectancy to purify my life and reorder my priorities so that I may continue in You. When You appear, I want with all my heart to be confident and unashamed before You at Your coming.[17] Please keep me focused on You.

    For the sake of the Bridegroom,
    And in His name—Jesus,
    Amen.

Beloved

The servant told Isaac all he had done. Isaac
brought her into the tent of his mother Sarah, and
he married Rebekah. So she became his wife, and
he loved her; and Isaac was comforted after his
mother's death.

—Genesis 24:66–67

A S THE SHADOWS DEEPENED ON THE DESERT TERRAIN,
Rebekah found herself gazing somewhat dimly
through the veil that now covered her face. The servant's master, this man, was the one who would be her
companion for life.

Isaac approached their camels. Rebekah's heart
must have raced with excitement as she saw his tan

face and dark eyes looking back at her with a warm welcome. When he drew nearer, one look at his awe-struck expression caused all her doubts and fears to vanish. She no longer wondered if she would be acceptable and beautiful in his eyes. She knew she was.

Standing quietly in the dusky twilight, she heard again the incredible story of answered prayer as the dear old servant told Isaac all that God had done on his journey to find a bride for him. The servant must have shared how God had led him to the very well from which Rebekah drew water. Once again, he related how he had asked God to reveal His chosen bride when she kindly gave him water and selflessly offered to water all his camels as well. As the servant filled Isaac in on the miraculous details, did Isaac's heart begin to beat loudly with anticipation of his imminent union with this wonderful woman, confident that God had prepared her for him? The love that had been growing in his heart at the thought of meeting her must have sent down roots into the very depths of his being. What joy he must have felt as he heard of the character and inner beauty of his soon-to-be bride. And surely Rebekah herself must have been humbled, honored, and thrilled all over again as the story was retold.

Then did Isaac's masculine voice ring out in the desert night air, announcing the arrival of the servant and the new bride? Did the quiet evening suddenly become a scene of bustling activity as servants hurried to prepare for her, eager to do their master's bidding? It may be that Rebekah saw the scurrying of the servants only in her peripheral vision, as her eyes surely must not have strayed from her bridegroom's face.

As she was ushered into what most likely was a tent compound and given a place to wash and put on clean clothing, I wonder if she was struck by the extravagance of her surroundings. Abraham was as wealthy as any desert king, so I expect woven carpets were on the ground, with rooms separated by linen curtains and each area filled with appropriate, well-placed embroidered cushions and comfortable furniture. And if luxurious silk clothing and spectacular jewelry had been carefully laid out for her, they would have confirmed that she had been expected, that preparations had been made long before her arrival. How her heart must have been warmed by the certainty that she was welcomed in Isaac's home. After her long journey, the comfort and beauty of her surroundings would have been a feast for her eyes. But perhaps the air was filled with savory aromas wafting through the compound, indicating that a celebration feast was sure to come. After she was able to settle in, I wonder if her maids were given rare perfumes and oils to pamper her and prepare her for her marriage.

As Rebekah entered the tent of Isaac's mother in the soft glow of the candlelight and was presented to Isaac, she would have finally known that she was loved. Genuinely, ardently, and beautifully loved by her long-awaited bridegroom. No more strenuous journey. No more waiting and hoping and wondering. No more doubts or feelings of inadequacy. She was the chosen bride, and Isaac loved her!

Have you, too, been on a long, difficult journey? Perhaps you are single but are longing for and dreaming of love. Maybe you are divorced, experiencing the deep hurt of rejection, bitter toward love and all its broken promises. Are you a widow, grieving the loss of your beloved, in despair over being separated from your sweet companion? Or maybe you are heartbroken in a loveless marriage, daily feeling the pain of being unloved. Perhaps the ache in your heart isn't related to your marital status. Maybe you struggle because your parents never told you they loved you. Or you struggle with a child who has rejected you and with whom you have lost contact. Or with a church that has removed you from membership. Or with estrangement from someone who had been your best friend. Sadly, any number of experiences can leave us feeling lost, lonely, and unloved.

Whatever journey you find yourself on today, dear precious bride of the King of kings, Jesus loves you. *He loves you!* Let there be no doubt in your mind. God has confirmed, "The LORD your God is with you, he is mighty to save. He will take great delight in you, he will quiet you with his love, he will rejoice over you with singing."[1] Therefore, "listen, O daughter, consider and give ear: Forget your people and your father's house. The king is enthralled by your beauty."[2]

As hard and long as your journey seems, one day it will be over. Jesus will come for you at your death,[3] and your faith will immediately become sight as you are ushered into His presence. Or if you are a member of the final generation, at any moment you may hear the trumpet blast and recognize the voice of the archangel as the sky unfolds and you are caught up in the air to see and live forever with the One who is your Bridegroom![4] The One who has been preparing a place for you and who has returned to take you to live with Him as His bride, just as He promised.[5]

One look at His face, and you will know you are infinitely loved! All your doubts and feelings of inadequacy will fade away. You will see the scars on His forehead where the crown of thorns dug deep and be reminded . . . you are loved! You will see the nail prints in His hands and feet and be reminded . . . you are loved! And you will know that your Savior is now Lord of the universe! He is right there! Before your eyes! In the flesh! You will hear Him call you by name as He welcomes you into His heavenly Home. As you gaze on your heavenly surroundings, you will become aware that you were expected. Your mansion will have been prepared with all the things He knows you like best— colors, music, landscape, flowers. You will be united with family members and friends who placed their faith in Jesus and arrived Home before you. Washed clean and clothed in a beautiful new robe of fine white linen,[6] you will be seated at the marriage feast of the Lamb.[7]

"Hallelujah! For our Lord God Almighty reigns. Let us rejoice and be glad and give him glory! For the wedding of the Lamb has come, and his bride has made herself ready."[8]

You are the King's beloved bride. He is waiting for you, preparing a place for you. Eagerly anticipating the electric moment when your faith becomes sight! Don't ever doubt. You have been chosen by the Father as the bride for His Son. You are loved. Loved! *Forever loved!*

DAY 21 CHALLENGE

Take a moment to close your eyes. Can you visualize the clouds of glory? Can you hear the universe reverberating with the praise of millions of angels singing, "Worthy is the Lamb"? As you are drawn into the presence of the One who is clothed in splendor and light . . . who stands in the center of the throne . . . who is worshipped by everything that has breath in the entire universe . . . the One who is the beloved only Son of the Father and who inherits all things . . . the One who is the most powerful, most important, most successful, wealthiest man in the universe . . . do you see His eyes searching the throngs of adoring angels until they rest on you? What does He see? What will He see?

Praise God! That moment has not yet come. There is still time to prepare. Still time to move your faith from salvation to transformation. Don't settle for just squeaking through the door of your heavenly Home. Instead, on this last day of our twenty-one-day challenge, commit to living your life from this moment forward so that you have an abundant welcome![9] Live your life so that five minutes before you see Him, you have no regrets, because you have made yourself ready, because you are a bride who confirms the Father's wisdom in choosing you, because you are worthy of His Son, the Bridegroom.

Lover of my soul,

    While my heart aches with longing to see You, the thought of the moment when I do see You puts this present moment in perspective. I am so humbly grateful that You have not come for me yet. There is still time to prepare. Please bring to my mind anything that is not pleasing to You. As I confess it, cleanse me of all my sin and imperfections. Clothe me in Your own spotless garments of righteousness. With all my heart, on that day, I want to be beautiful in Your eyes.

    For the sake of You, my Bridegroom,
    And in Your name—Jesus,
    Amen.

Preparing to Meet Jesus

EVERY YEAR, OUR FAMILY SPENDS TIME AT THE BEACH in the summer. For more than fifty years, we have kept up this annual trek, which has become a much-anticipated family vacation. Even though my husband, Danny, is now in Heaven on permanent "vacation," and even though not everyone can come for the entire time because of school, sports, and work schedules, everyone will come for at least some of the time.

While it is lots of fun, I'm always amazed by how much I have to do to get ready to leave. Days before-hand, my daughters and I plan out the menus and gro-cery lists. We all share in making casseroles in advance to help with the actual meals once we arrive. I make lists of things to take like clothes, beach chairs, fans, an ice cream freezer, DVDs for the kids, books, sun-screen, games—the lists go on and on. And then, of course, comes the day I actually pack the pickup truck, checking my lists again and again to make sure I haven't forgotten anything. By the time I arrive at the beach, I assure you, I'm more than ready for a vacation!

All the above makes me think that if it requires about ten days of detailed, intentional preparation just to get ready for a family vacation, surely every moment of the time we have left on earth is necessary to pre-pare us to meet Jesus and live with Him forever in His heavenly Home. Which, of course, is why Rachel-Ruth and I are writing this book together. We need to remind ourselves—and you—of the conscientious preparation necessary if we are to be a bride that is pleasing both to the Father and to His Son.

As Jesus sat with His disciples on the Mount of Olives, overlooking the city of Jerusalem, He empha-sized the necessity of being prepared to meet Him when He returns. While He clearly stated that no one would know the day or the hour of His return, the signs He gave were specific enough to help His disci-ples pinpoint the generation.[1]

Based on what Jesus said and what I see happen-ing in our world today, I believe we are living in the last generation. At any moment the sky will roll back, a loud trumpet blast will sound, the voice of the archangel will ring out, and the Son of God Himself will descend with a commanding victory shout to call His bride Home.[2]

Jesus used a story to help His disciples grasp the critical significance of being ready for that moment:

> At that time the kingdom of heaven will be like ten virgins who took their lamps and went out to meet the bridegroom. Five of them were foolish and five were wise. The foolish ones took their lamps but did not take any oil with them. The wise, however, took oil in jars along with their lamps. The bridegroom was a long time in coming, and they all became drowsy and fell asleep.
>
> At midnight the cry rang out: "Here's the bridegroom! Come out to meet him!"
>
> Then all the virgins woke up and trimmed their lamps. The foolish ones said to the wise, "Give us some of your oil; our lamps are going out."
>
> "No," they replied, "there may not be enough for both us and you. Instead, go to those who sell oil and buy some for yourselves."
>
> But while they were on their way to buy the oil, the bridegroom arrived. The virgins who were ready went in with him to the wedding banquet. And the door was shut.

Later the others also came. "Sir! Sir!" they said. "Open the door for us!"

But he replied, "I tell you the truth, I don't know you."

Therefore keep watch, because you do not know the day or the hour.[3]

The Anticipation

The fact that Jesus is coming for His bride isn't debatable. As we've already learned, He will come for us in one of two ways. Either He will come for us at our death, or He will come for us at what is referred to as the Rapture—when believers will be caught up to meet Him in the air, as Paul described in 1 Thessalonians 4. It's this second event that is on my mind as we conclude this book. While old age or infirmity may alert us that our physical death is near, the return of Jesus at the Rapture will occur suddenly, with no warning beyond the signs given in Scripture. How do I know? Because He said so! And He is the truth. He clearly stated that He would come again to receive us to Himself.[4] If I believe what He said about sin, salvation, forgiveness, the love of God the Father, eternal life, His own identity, and all the other foundational truths,[5] then it stands to reason that what He said about His return is equally true. Jesus is coming! "The glorious appearing of our great God and Savior, Jesus Christ" is imminent![6]

We live in a world filled with blasphemy, obscenity, profanity, and outright rebellion against God; a world that is morally, spiritually, and environmentally filthy; a world of selfishness, greed, pride, and abuse; a world where the family unit is being destroyed;[7] a world of hate, rage, lies, corruption, cruelty, confusion, lawlessness, and delusion. But make no mistake: Our blessed hope is that a new world is coming! Even now it is being prepared as a Home for the Son's bride. And when all preparations are complete, He will come, whether or not we are ready.

The ten young women in Jesus's story had several things in common: Each had a lamp, which represents a profession of faith. Each believed and expected that the bridegroom was coming. Eventually, all grew so tired of waiting when he seemed to tarry that they went to sleep.

But there was also one life-changing, destiny-altering difference: Five of the young women had oil for their lamps, and five of the young women had none. Throughout Scripture, oil represents the Holy Spirit. In other words, half of those waiting for the bridegroom's coming were ready because they had a personal relationship with Jesus and were indwelt by the Holy Spirit, while the other half had only a profession of faith. They looked the part, they were religious, but they had no oil—no indwelling of the Holy Spirit. They had never been born again. Jesus said earlier that while some people may know His Word, they don't live it out.[8] The apostle Paul described such people as "having a form of godliness but denying its power."[9] In His story, Jesus called them "foolish."

To be honest, it can be very difficult for you and me to tell the difference between wise and foolish people, between those who have an authentic relationship with God through faith in Jesus and those who are simply outwardly religious. Jesus told this story not to prompt us to speculate about or be judgmental of others but to stir us to examine our own hearts. From His point of view, are we wise or foolish? Do we have the oil of the indwelling Holy Spirit or not?

The Awakening

As we've seen, after waiting and waiting and waiting for the bridegroom, all ten young women grew so tired that they went to sleep. But then they were awakened by the midnight cry. Was it an earthquake?[10] Was it the start of a world war? Was it a famine?[11] Was it a series of blood moons or solar eclipses?[12] Was it the loud voice of the archangel and the blast of the heavenly trumpet?[13] While no one knows for sure what the midnight cry represents, we know something got the attention of all who were waiting. And they all recognized it as a signal that the bridegroom was on his way.

But this is where the critical difference between the young women was revealed. Five had oil for their lamps, and five did not. When those with no oil asked the others to share, they were refused. While their response sounds harsh and uncaring, it actually was an impossible request. No one can give the oil of the Holy Spirit to another person. You and I must receive the oil for ourselves when we confess our sin, turn away from our sin, claim Jesus as our Savior, and surrender to Him as Lord. We then open our hearts and invite Him to come into us, which He does in the person of the Holy Spirit. As Rachel-Ruth explained in the very first chapter, this is when we become a member of the Father's family. And it's this indwelling of the Holy Spirit—the oil in your lamp—that makes all the difference when the Bridegroom comes.

The Arrival

Once the midnight cry sounded, the bridegroom arrived. The five young women who were waiting with oil in their lamps went in with him to the wedding feast. The other five had gone off to buy oil, and when they returned, the door to the wedding festivities was shut. When they demanded that it be opened, the bridegroom told them he didn't know them.

Our world seems to be experiencing repeated alarms indicating that at any moment the midnight cry may sound and Jesus will return. Wars, rumors of wars, earthquakes, famines, signs in the heavens—all are getting our attention. At any moment the Bridegroom is going to arrive. When He comes, He will come suddenly. Quickly. With no further advance notice.[14] Those who have the oil—the seal—of the indwelling Holy Spirit will go with Him to the Home He has prepared for His bride.[15] Those who don't will be shut out of Heaven because He doesn't know them in a personal relationship.[16] While they have had a lamp of profession or religion, they never established a personal relationship with Him.

Be honest. Which is true of you? I can't tell. Only you and the Bridegroom know for sure.

It's imperative that you and I not wait to get ready. We need to *be* ready. Since no one knows the day or the hour of His arrival, He instructs us again and again to watch for Him.[17] We watch by staying informed about the world situation, taking note of the signs Jesus gave as we read our Bibles.[18]

As you wait and watch, there are four things you can do to be ready for His coming.

First and foremost, make sure that you have oil in

your lamp. Make sure that you know Jesus in a personal relationship and that He knows you as one who has put your trust in Him as Savior and Lord.

Second, maintain moment-by-moment surrender to the moment-by-moment control of the indwelling Holy Spirit so that you are continuing to be conformed to the image of Jesus.[19] Use the characteristics of Rebekah that Rachel-Ruth pulled out in this book as a checklist for your own character. Then ask God to help you develop the ones you are deficient in and strengthen the others. Because while we can't take things with us to Heaven, we will take our character.

Third, make Jesus attractive and desirable to others by the way you live and by what you say and do. Share the gospel clearly so that people know they can claim Jesus as their Savior, receive Him as their Lord, and look forward to Heaven as their Home. Explain to them the necessity of receiving the oil now, before the Bridegroom comes. How thrilling it will be when we gather around the throne in Heaven and see people who are there because of what we shared with them here.

And fourth, reorder your priorities so that when the midnight cry goes out, you will have no regrets for the way you have lived from this moment forward. So . . .

Get ready! Don't procrastinate. Prepare now to meet Jesus face-to-face. The Bridegroom *is* coming!

NOTES

Introduction: The One the Father Seeks

1. Galatians 2:20.
2. Matthew 9:15; 25:1–13.
3. Revelation 19:9.
4. Ephesians 5:25–27; 2 Peter 3:14.
5. "Genesis 24:10," *John Gill's Exposition of the Bible*, Bible Study Tools, accessed October 28, 2022, www.bible studytools.com/commentaries/gills-exposition-of-the-bible/genesis-24-10.html.
6. Genesis 24:2.
7. Genesis 15:2.
8. Genesis 24:3–4.
9. Genesis 24:5.
10. Genesis 24:7.
11. Genesis 24:8.
12. Genesis 24:10.
13. Genesis 24:11.
14. Some translations substitute "spring" for "well."
15. Genesis 16:7–13; 21:14–19.
16. Genesis 29:1–12.

17. Exodus 2:15–22.
18. Judges 7:1–8.
19. John 4:14.
20. John 7:38–39.
21. John 4:28–30.
22. Isaiah 12:3.
23. Genesis 24:12–14.
24. Genesis 24:17.
25. Genesis 24:19.
26. Genesis 24:23.
27. Genesis 24:24.
28. Genesis 24:27.
29. Genesis 24:29–30.
30. Genesis 24:31.
31. Genesis 24:33.
32. Genesis 24:35.
33. Genesis 24:36.
34. Genesis 24:37–38.
35. Genesis 24:40.
36. Genesis 24:48.
37. Genesis 24:49.
38. Genesis 24:50–51.
39. Genesis 24:52.
40. Genesis 24:56.
41. Genesis 24:58.
42. Genesis 24:58.
43. Genesis 24:61.
44. Genesis 21:1–7.
45. Genesis 21:8–21.
46. Genesis 22:1–18.
47. John 14:26.
48. Luke 1:26–38; 2:6–7.
49. Luke 7:22.
50. John 19:17–30.
51. Matthew 28:1–7.
52. Acts 1:9–11.
53. Hebrews 1:2.
54. 2 Thessalonians 2:14.
55. 1 Corinthians 12:7–11; Hebrews 2:3–4.

56. Hebrews 1:3; 7:25.
57. John 14:3.
58. 1 Peter 1:8.
59. Genesis 24:65.
60. Genesis 24:65.
61. Genesis 24:65.
62. Genesis 24:66.
63. Genesis 24:67.
64. John 14:23.
65. Revelation 19:7.

Day 1: A Family Member

1. Genesis 24:4.
2. John 1:11.
3. John 1:12.
4. Genesis 24:8.

Day 2: Faithful in the Day-to-Day

1. 1 Thessalonians 5:2.
2. Zechariah 14:20–21.
3. Exodus 3:1–10.
4. Judges 6:11–16.
5. Luke 5:1–11; Acts 10.
6. John 4:4–26.
7. Luke 10:38–42; John 11:1–44.
8. Matthew 25:21.
9. Ecclesiastes 9:10.

Day 3: Beautiful . . . on the Inside

1. Galatians 5:22–23.
2. 1 Samuel 16:7.
3. 1 Samuel 16:12.
4. 1 Samuel 16:12.

5. Acts 16:16–34.
6. Revelation 1:9–18.
7. Acts 7:55–60.
8. Jeremiah 38:1–13.
9. Hosea 1:2–3; 3:1–3.

Day 4: Purified

1. Hebrews 9:14.
2. Psalm 32:3; Matthew 24:12.
3. Revelation 2;4.
4. Psalm 66:18.
5. 1 Corinthians 6:9–11.
6. Revelation 21:5.
7. Isaiah 57:15.
8. 2 Peter 3:14.
9. Psalm 51:8, 12.
10. 1 John 1:7.

Day 5: Spiritually Filled

1. Isaiah 27:3, NKJV.
2. Isaiah 55:10–11.
3. Psalm 121:7–8.
4. John 4:10, 13–14.
5. Revelation 22:17.

Day 6: Kind

1. Colossians 3:12.
2. 2 Timothy 3:1–5.
3. Corrie ten Boom, *The Hiding Place* (Grand Rapids, Mich.: Chosen Books, 2006), 203–14.
4. 2 Corinthians 1:3–4.
5. 1 Thessalonians 5:11; Hebrews 3:13.

Day 7: A Humble Servant

1. Sarah Crupi, "Truth or Tail: A Camel's Hump," Cleveland Zoological Society, April 6, 2021, www.clevelandzoosociety .org/z/2021/04/06/truth-or-tail-a-camels-hump.
2. Genesis 24:14.
3. Mark 9:35.
4. John 13:15.
5. Philippians 2:3–5.
6. Philippians 2:6–9.
7. Ephesians 1:22.

Day 8: Responsive to Needs

1. John 7:38.
2. John 5:6.

Day 9: Honest

1. Matthew 24:8, 12.
2. 2 Corinthians 8:21.
3. Daniel 6:4–5.
4. Revelation 1:14.
5. Psalm 139:1–4, 23–24.

Day 10: Motivated

1. Colossians 3:23–24.
2. Revelation 22:12.
3. Matthew 16:27.
4. Matthew 5:12.
5. Matthew 5:46.
6. Matthew 6:1–4.
7. Matthew 6:5–6, 16–18.
8. Matthew 10:42.
9. 1 Corinthians 2:9.

Day 11: Unashamed

1. Matthew 10:32–33.
2. John 13:38.
3. Mark 14:31.
4. Mark 14:66–72.
5. John 21:15–17.
6. Hebrews 1:1–3.
7. Ephesians 1:20–22.
8. John 5:22–27.
9. Gary Lane, "Nigeria Miracle: Boko Haram Victim Habila Adamu," CBN, accessed November 2, 2022, www1.cbn .com/globallane-56.
10. "Nigerian Christian Shot in Face by Boko Haram, Survives Attack," The Voice of the Martyrs, October 1, 2014, www .persecution.com/stories/nigerian-christian-shot-by-boko -haram.

Day 12: Hospitable

1. Romans 12:13.
2. 1 Peter 4:9.
3. Matthew 10:40.
4. 2 Kings 4:10.
5. Hebrews 13:1–2.

Day 13: Eager to Share

1. Psalm 66:16.
2. Romans 1:8, 12.
3. 2 Corinthians 9:1–2.
4. Mark 16:11; John 20:1–2, 10–18.

Day 14: Authentic

1. Matthew 23:27–28.
2. Matthew 23:13, 15, 16, 23, 25, 27, 29.

3. Romans 12:9.
4. Hebrews 1:3.
5. John 1:18.

Day 15: A Good Listener

1. Philippians 4:6–7, emphasis added.
2. Isaiah 41:10.
3. Genesis 6–8.
4. Genesis 41–47.
5. Exodus 3–14.
6. Joshua 6.
7. 2 Samuel 7–16.
8. Nehemiah 8–10.
9. Acts 9.
10. Revelation 1; 21–22.
11. Revelation 2:7, 11, 17, 29; 3:6, 13, 22.
12. The two churches that did listen are Smyrna (modern-day Izmir) and Philadelphia (modern-day Alaşehir), both of which exist today in Turkey.
13. 1 Kings 19:11–12.
14. Ezekiel 1:24–25.

Day 16: Submissive

1. Ephesians 5:21–6:9.
2. Joshua 1:9.
3. Romans 8:28. Our ultimate good isn't to be healthy, wealthy, happy, or problem-free. Our ultimate good is to be conformed to the image of Jesus Christ.
4. Matthew 26:39.
5. Romans 3:23–26.
6. Psalm 118:7.
7. Psalm 51:10.
8. Ezekiel 36:26.
9. John 13:13–15, 17.

Day 17: A Blessing to Others

1. 1 Peter 3:8–9.
2. 1 Samuel 25:3.
3. 1 Samuel 25:35.
4. Matthew 5:44–45.
5. Matthew 5:11–12.
6. Galatians 5:22–23.
7. Revelation 22:1–2.

Day 18: Committed

1. Genesis 3.
2. Genesis 4:1–16.
3. Genesis 16:1–12.
4. Acts 5:1–10.
5. Exodus 7–12.
6. 1 Samuel 17:1–54.
7. Daniel 3:1–29.
8. Daniel 6:1–27.
9. Acts 16:16–34.
10. Matthew 16:24–25.
11. 2 Corinthians 3:18.
12. 2 Timothy 1:12.

Day 19: Perseverant

1. Genesis 24:54–59.
2. Genesis 24:59.
3. Genesis 16:13.
4. Genesis 12:1–5.
5. Genesis 22:1–12.
6. 1 John 2:28.
7. Revelation 2:1–7.
8. Hebrews 7:25.

Day 20: Focused

1. Genesis 12:6–7.
2. Genesis 17–18.
3. Genesis 13:1–4.
4. Genesis 22:1–2.
5. Genesis 23:19.
6. Genesis 19:23–25.
7. Genesis 24:65.
8. Mrs. Charles E. Cowman, *Streams in the Desert* (Grand Rapids, Mich.: Zondervan, 1996), March 27 reading.
9. John 17.
10. John 17:15.
11. 1 Peter 1:8.
12. Matthew 24:36.
13. 1 Thessalonians 4:16–18, emphasis added.
14. Matthew 24:43–44.
15. Hebrews 12:2.
16. Matthew 24:42.
17. 1 John 2:28.

Day 21: Beloved

1. Zephaniah 3:17.
2. Psalm 45:10–11.
3. 2 Corinthians 5:6–8.
4. 1 Thessalonians 4:15–17.
5. John 14:2–3.
6. Revelation 7:9–14; 19:7–8.
7. Revelation 19:9.
8. Revelation 19:6–7.
9. 2 Peter 1:11.

Epilogue: Preparing to Meet Jesus

1. Matthew 24.
2. 1 Thessalonians 4:16–18.

3. Matthew 25:1–13.
4. John 14:3; Revelation 22:20.
5. John 3:16–17; 5:17–21; 11:25–26.
6. Titus 2:13.
7. 2 Timothy 3:1–4.
8. Matthew 7:26–27.
9. 2 Timothy 3:5.
10. Revelation 6:12–14.
11. Matthew 24:7.
12. Luke 21:25; Acts 2:19–20.
13. 1 Thessalonians 4:16.
14. Zephaniah 1:14; 1 Corinthians 15:51–52; 1 Thessalonians 5:1–3.
15. Ephesians 1:13–14.
16. Matthew 7:21–23.
17. Matthew 24:42, 44.
18. Matthew 24:1–14, 32–41.
19. 2 Corinthians 3:18.

ABOUT THE AUTHORS

Called "the best preacher in the family" by her late father, Billy Graham, ANNE GRAHAM LOTZ speaks around the globe with the wisdom and authority of years spent studying God's Word.

The New York Times named Anne one of the five most influential evangelists of her generation. Her Just Give Me Jesus revivals have been held in more than thirty cities in twelve countries, with hundreds of thousands of attendees.

Anne is a bestselling and award-winning author of twenty books. She is the president of AnGeL Ministries in Raleigh, North Carolina, and served as chairperson of the National Day of Prayer Task Force from 2016 to 2017.

Whether a delegate to the World Economic Forum's annual meeting, a commentator in *The Washington Post,* or a groundbreaking speaker on platforms throughout the world, Anne's aim is clear: to bring revival to the hearts of God's people. And her message is consistent: calling people into a personal relationship with God through His Word.

RACHEL-RUTH LOTZ WRIGHT is a graduate of Baylor University. She is married to Steven Wright, a high school football head coach, and they have three wonderful teenage daughters, who have given her a heart for children and for those who raise them. God opened the door for her to speak at schools, churches, and other venues across the country to share the gospel with kids and also to ignite in parents a desire to raise disciples who love God's Word.

For over ten years, Rachel-Ruth has been teaching a weekly Bible study, which is now online and draws a global audience of thousands. It is her desire that people, no matter their age, would be drawn into a vibrant love relationship with the Lord through His Word.

Rachel-Ruth holds the position of ministry teaching associate at AnGeL Ministries, serves on the AnGeL Ministries board of directors, and chairs the weekly prayer team that undergirds her mother's ministry. Rachel-Ruth and her family live in Raleigh, North Carolina.

ANNE GRAHAM LOTZ

ANGEL MINISTRIES

5115 Hollyridge Drive

Raleigh, NC 27612-3111

(919) 787-6606

info@AnneGrahamLotz.org

Faith is relayed from generation to generation

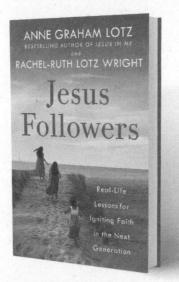

With inspiring stories from their family and practical insights, this engaging book from Billy Graham's daughter and granddaughter gives us a glimpse of an enduring legacy of faith and equips us to raise Jesus Followers of our own.

Available from waterbrookmultnomah.com

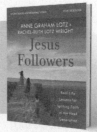

Join the authors for a five-session study as they demonstrate a family Bible study discussion, plus four ways to ignite faith in the next generation, centered around your witness, worship, walk, and work.

Available from churchsource.com

OPEN YOUR HEART
TO GOD'S INVITATION
TO PRAYER

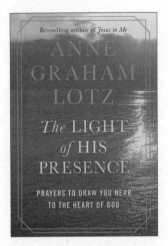

Why is it that as soon as we bow our heads to pray, we start thinking of other things we need to do? How do we make time to pray in the middle of our busy lives? And how do we know what to say and how to say it?

Like many of us, Anne Graham Lotz has struggled with prayer. Over the years, she discovered that writing out her prayers draws her into deeper, more intimate conversations with God. *The Light of His Presence* offers forty of these tender, honest prayers for real-life situations as an invitation to deepen your own prayer life through worship, confession, thanksgiving, and intercession. You'll be encouraged to lean more fully into God's promises through this power-packed devotional resource, which includes inspiring quotes from Christians throughout the ages and also has space to journal your own words to God.

As Anne writes, "My prayer for you as you read this volume is that God will use my struggle with prayer to help you overcome yours. And that, as a result, you will be drawn nearer to the heart of God."

waterbrookmultnomah.com

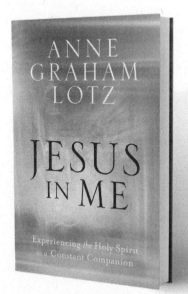